Shipping Address:
Edward P. Wilson
10 Argyle Lane
Apt. 205
Gabriola, B.C. V0R 1X0
Canada

Item Price	Total
$11.95	$11.95

$11.95
$6.48
$18.43
$18.43
$0.00

For detailed information about this and other orders, please visit Your Account. You can also print invoices, change your e-mail address and payment settings, alter your communication preferences, and much more – 24 hours a day – at http://www.amazon.com/your-account.

Returns Are Easy!

Visit http://www.amazon.com/returns to return any item – including gifts – in unopened or original condition within 30 days for a full refund (other restrictions apply). Please have your order ID ready.

Thanks for shopping at Amazon.com, and please come again!

amazon.com.

amazon.com.

Amazon.com
1850 Mercer Rd.
Lexington, KY 40511

Edward P. Wilson
500 Argyle Lane
Apt. 205
Gabriola, B.C. V0R 1X0
Canada

Billing Address:
Edward P. Wilson
500 Argyle Lane
Apt. 205
Gabriola, B.C. V0R 1X0
Canada

qhvt52117/-1-/std-intl-us-ca/2631493 1S

Your order of February 17, 2006 (Order ID 103-9720862-5053419)

Qty.	Item
	IN THIS SHIPMENT
1	Greed : A treatise in two essays Edney, Julian --- Paperback (** P-1-G8E169 **) 0595360009

Subtotal
Shipping & Handling
Order Total
Paid via Visa
Balance due

This shipment completes your order.

41/qhvt52117/-1-//1S/std-intl-us-ca/2631493/0220-14:00/0220-05:21/tott   Pack Type: BCLIB (12X9X

GREED

GREED

◆

A treatise in two essays

Julian Edney

iUniverse, Inc.
New York Lincoln Shanghai

GREED
A treatise in two essays

Copyright © 2005 by Julian Edney

All rights reserved. No part of this book may be used or reproduced by any means, graphic, electronic, or mechanical, including photocopying, recording, taping or by any information storage retrieval system without the written permission of the publisher except in the case of brief quotations embodied in critical articles and reviews.

iUniverse books may be ordered through booksellers or by contacting:

iUniverse
2021 Pine Lake Road, Suite 100
Lincoln, NE 68512
www.iuniverse.com
1-800-Authors (1-800-288-4677)

ISBN-13: 978-0-595-36000-0 (pbk)
ISBN-13: 978-0-595-80451-1 (ebk)
ISBN-10: 0-595-36000-9 (pbk)
ISBN-10: 0-595-80451-9 (ebk)

Printed in the United States of America

Contents

GREED 1
GREED II 30
    THE NUTS GAME 70
    NOTES: GREED 73
    NOTES: GREED II 78
    NOTES: THE NUTS GAME 83

GREED

An essay concerning the origins, nature, extent and morality of this destructive force in free market economies. Definitions. Paradoxes and omissions in Adam Smith's original theory permit—encourage—greed without restraint so that in a very large society over two centuries it has become an undemocratic force creating precipitous inequalities; divisions in this society now approach a kind of wealth apartheid, and our values are quite unlike Smith's: this is an immensely wealthy society but it is not a humane society. Wealth and poverty are connected, in fact recent sociological theory shows our institutions routinely design inequality in, but this connection is largely avoided in texts and in the media, as is the notion that greed is a moral wrong. Problems created by greed cannot be solved by technology. We are also distracted by already-outdated environmental rhetoric, arguments that scarcities and human suffering follow from abuse of our ecology. Rather, these scarcities are the result of what people do to people. This focus opens practical solutions (1).

Sign the tab in certain Midtown eateries and your neighbors' eyes slide over. Is that a $48,000 Michel Perchin pen? What's on your wrist—a $300,000 Breguet watch?

In Palm Springs and Bel Air, $100,000 twin-turbo Porsches and $225,000 Ferraris buzz the warm streets. In New York at an exclusive Morell & Company auction last May, a single magnum of Dom Perignon champagne was sold for $5,750. And there are the paintings of course—one evening at auction two Monets sold for $43 million (2). Hotel rooms, anyone, at $10,000 a night? Estate agents in suburbs of Dallas and Palm Beach have advertised baronial homes for sale at over $40 million (3).

These are prices paid by the exceptionally wealthy, the folks who skim the pages of the *Robb Report* (average annual salary of subscribers: $1.2 million) in whose glossy pages are reviewed the best of everything. In a recent issue a southern plantation is advertised, "everybody's dream," at $8.5 million.

Robert Reich points out that the superrich live in a parallel universe to the rest of the country: much of the time we don't see them because they live in walled estates, travel in private limousines and use different airports from the rest of us (4). There's lots of them. There are now more than 200 billionaires. Some five percent of American households have assets over $1 million. And we're back to levels of extravagant consumption not seen for 100 years *(5)*.

By historical accounts this is a nation of persistent and resilient people with an unshakable mission: the pursuit of happiness. This idea of happiness is largely connected with wealth (and this connection has long philosophic roots). It is a nation of ambitious people with notions of unfettered future growth, a nation that celebrates abundance. There seems to be no reason anyone should be deprived of luxury, if he works hard. Indeed with this country's aggregate wealth, there should be no reason anyone should ever go hungry or suffer.

People are going hungry in America. A Los Angeles survey found more than a quarter of low income residents, many working, are not getting enough food to meet basic nutritional needs. And 10% are experiencing hunger *(6)*.

Estimates are that 3 out of 10 Americans will face poverty sometime in their lives *(7)*.

Misery is a word seldom applied to the contemporary scene. Like wretchedness it seems antique, an Old World term. But many Americans live in cold, dank slums; many do not earn enough for shelter, many sleep outside. In America's inner cities and at its lowest levels, under freeway bridges and in tubercular alleys, in stained and broken rooming houses and in torn-apart schools, misery exists and persists. All our largest cities contain neighborhoods where some people live day to day in apartments that could be mistaken for closets, some fearing to leave home on gang-terrorized streets, some sharing bus seats with people with drug-scarred arms. Every great metropolis has its skid row mired in fecal gutters, where whole blocks are awash in narcotics and violence, its inhabitants despised and flatly abandoned.

America is once again a nation of extremes.

Sealed Off

As this society grows, it becomes more unequal. As aggregate wealth goes up, equality goes down. Our population has soared 13.2% in the last decade alone to 281 million *(8)*, and the wealth has been concentrating in fewer hands (it has since the 1770s *(9)*) and the difference between the richest and the poorest is now immense. While the wealthiest individuals count their assets in the tens of billions, the lowest classes are falling. Americans' earnings are more unequal today than they have been any time in the past 60 years *(10)*. Some corporations' CEOs have been making over 400 times the hourly rate of their lowest worker *(11)* but this inequality is not just a feature of businesses, it spans a variety of professions, perhaps to include my favorite musicians and your favorite athletes. For example, shortstop Alex Rodriguez's $252 million 10 year baseball contract pays him $170,000 per game *(12)*. To a person receiving the average allocation of $83 per month in food stamps, the inequality is astronomical, and the chances of closing it so small it doesn't feel like a real freedom.

If the best-off are sealing themselves off, the worst-off are also doubly fenced about, this time by the distrust and aversion of those above. Around 20% of American children are living in poverty. An estimated two million are homeless some time during the year *(13)*, including whole families and people who have full- or part-time jobs *(14)*.

This is a flamboyantly optimistic and self-congratulatory society, and the puzzle is why it allows this suffering. The inequalities are stunning, but a frequent attitude is a shrug—so what?. These days it is hard to plumb a concern.

Frequently I survey acquaintances with this touchstone question, attributed to Rawls *(15)*: Suppose there are people living on one side of a big city who throw weekly parties so lavish that afterwards they are throwing out meat, while on the other side of the same town are people so poor they cannot afford to buy meat at all. Is this a moral problem?

I get a spectrum of answers: "No problem" to "Yes, of course" and in between "Technological, but not ethical problem," and "Maybe, but (horrified look) what solution are you pushing?"—as well as some yawns, as if these questions were so old fashioned. I believe the variety of these responses eventually leads to the question of what kind of society we live in.

Winner Takes All

My first point is that these extremes of wealth are connected. While the rich are growing richer, the poor are growing poorer *(16)*, and this is no coincidence. But we largely deny the connection. This is a society which, as the divide between the happy and the abject grows, tries, now by education, now by medication, now by paradox, now by distraction, to avoid the inhuman consequences of its collective actions, and in the end—because none of those strategies is effective—it is one that uses specific strategies for vacating reality.

Defenders, of course, argue that the rich getting richer benefits all, and that in an economy that is an unlimited, growing, open system, all can rise, that (once we get through temporary difficulties) we will find a full and abundant world.

In fact these are not so much arguments as swollen cliches.

There is indeed a problem, and it has a history. I will sift the philosophy of utilitarianism and Adam Smith's founding economics theory for origins. Smith's 1776 treatise, we recall, tied the growth of wealth to the work of common entrepreneurs. It refused the inherited inequalities of aristocracy and with the Enlightenment's notion of reason, a quality accessible to Everyman, it promptly democratized the economy. This philosophy was exported whole cloth to the new America, and it has since grown to dominate our economic policies, its influence is now worldwide. But despite its original claims, we will find it woven with mystical filaments and contradictions. I will show that as the theory is commonly related, it is hard to separate rationality from dogma.

Competition is a fundamental good in utilitarian economics. Competition is a process which results in inequalities—winners and losers. It cannot be, in a society of free competitive units, that competition among all is good for all. Modern analysts Cook and Frank show free market competition has become so stark that we are becoming a winner-takes-all society [17]. In a giant economy, aggressive acquisition, greed, where so widespread and popular as to be celebrated, has resulted in colossal differences, so that, as much as we are accustomed to reproaching the Europeans for their inequalities, we are now caught in a lie. We have become more unequal. The United States is the wealthiest nation. But its 20.3 percent child poverty rate ranks worse than all European nations [18].

Historians Will and Ariel Durant [19] estimated in their survey that the gap between the wealthiest and the poorest in America has become greater than at any time since Imperial plutocratic Rome.

Paradoxes

Inequality is a non-issue to the defenders of Smithian economics. The pursuit of excellence makes it inevitable and, they argue, the pursuit of excellence benefits all. So we are hostage to a paradox. As powerfully as we struggle for wealth and happiness we fling ourselves on the axiom that we all are equal, leaving some damage to the national psyche.

The whispered truth is that this nation bent on the pursuit of happiness is not so happy. Suicide afflicts all classes, and suicide rates are now so high as to eclipse homicide rates with three suicides for every two murders. Surgeon General Satcher partially blamed the media [20]. Clinical depression is at its highest rate in decades [21]. There are unprecedented rates of anxiety, companionship itself is receding, trust is fading [22]. Tens of millions are using prescription mood elevators.

Scarcity oppresses. And the worst signs of unhappiness cluster in the lowest cuts: we have among the highest national rates of imprisonment, and the Administration concedes there are 5 million hard-core drug users in America [23] and millions of alcoholics, all disproportionately among the poor.

Resonating with the battle cry of the French Revolution, *Liberte, Egalite, Fraternite*, the American Constitution was written with promises of human liberty and equality. Freedom and equality qualify as the fundamental political virtues. They are the two legs upon which democracy walks.

The second of the promises is broken.

So we first have a philosophical problem: There are many reasons for inequality, but it is ensured in an unfettered materialistic society by a celebrated style of acquisition we call greed. Greed is not just the whimsical excess of the individual. Its most virulent forms are displayed by business groups and corporations—but aggregated, it is an antidemocratic force.

Greed demolishes equity. Simply, you cannot have both unrestrained greed and equality.

Apartheid Economy

The principle of freedom always comes first, argues the Smithian capitalist. But in America, freedom has become something else, a wild individualism (24) with a strange amnesia—a disconnect between parts of our culture. A kind of sociopathic haze is settling, helped by mood-altering drugs and television, and appearing in the fashionable cluelessness and chic ignorance—so ubiquitous they have aerated society to numbness. Another facet is the narcissism (to rival one of Dostoevsky's characters so narcissistic he cared more about an ounce of his own body fat than the lives of 100,000 of his own countrymen (25)). What the free individual chooses to do is now paramount, and the poor understand that detachment is the pivot. Detachment allows the paradox that you can both compete with others but not be involved with what results. The concept of "the common good" has almost disappeared, and nobody is his brother's keeper.

Neither are these inequalities an unfortunate by-product of the healthy struggle. Competitive acquisition for the sake of exhibition is again in vogue—and it seems television repeatedly flaunts that on the way to wealth, there are no principles competitors won't compromise. Besides hunger and fear, lack of health care, decent education and housing shortages, which make living hard, the poor live with brash opulence in their faces. People in decaying buildings daily watch glittering television scenes of shining cars, ocean yachts, and overflowing parties of the rich and famous. Owned by these images, a poor person cannot but feel the differences, and year by year these images add a sedimented frustration, resentment, sense of failure and inferiority which they cannot avoid.

Poverty is also punitive. The poverty-struck family is not just paying the price of its own failure: it is also paying the price of others' success.

Still, many regard these problems as if they were no more than the economy's stubble, moles, and split ends.

Second, we have a practical problem. The Durants show a cycle repeating through history. Great social inequality creates an unstable equilibrium. The swelling numbers of the poor and resentful come to rival the power of the rich. As grievances and restlessness grow, government worsens, becoming tyrannical. Eventually a critical point arrives. Wealth will be redistributed, either by politics, or by revolution.

Denying the Shadow

Could it happen in America? To some analysts, it is already beginning. A survey released by the Milton S. Eisenhower Foundation attributes our enduring levels of violence to "vast and shameful inequality in income, wealth and opportunity among urban poor" who are often "trapped in places of terror" [26]—inequalities which are simply un-American, opines C. Murphy [27]. Troubling studies exist, but we surround this research with technicians questioning methodology and politicians arguing the study represents no reality. There is denial: "Forget the data," asserts one newspaper columnist on poverty issues, "…things have gotten better." [28]

Finally, this issue is no longer the environmentalist's concern about scarcity of natural resources, nor the population expert's warnings about Earth's limits to growth. These scarcities are man made, the result of what people do to people. The fact is, far from being an abundant world, it is a world of scarcity because we calibrate it so. And yet the moral connection is absent.

Currently our aggregate wealth is like a high tide, covering many unpleasant things on the ocean floor. When there is full employment, we all seem happily raised. But a few years ago the *Harvard Business Review* carried an article daring to look down: Richard Freeman [29] warns that under the surface America is becoming dangerously segregated, forming an apartheid economy, and the lowest are not free to move up. Freeman adds a shadow. He sketches in a huge new group of Americans, the economically sinking workers who are trailing their counterparts in other advanced countries.

Sociologist Derber's point is that where people are homeless, starving, or jobless, civil society has failed [30].

But these demographics will not reverse, because we are a society busily denying its own shadow. In this essay I will pull back the curtain on the irrational in this driving, powerful economy. Instead of an overarching machinery running on smooth technical devices, we shall see a clutter of denial, rationalization, visionary statements and internal contradictions. And the quietness around this topic has another reason. Perhaps we had better be quiet. If we look up, we see Goliath.

Definitions

Greed vastly predates Smithian economics, of course. It is one of the Bible's Seven Deadly Sins. Contemporary dictionaries define it as intense acquisitiveness of (usually material) goods or wealth. To dilate: *Greed* is the acquisition of a desirable good by one person or a group beyond need, resulting in unequal distribution to the point others are deprived. *Competitive greed* is the same type of acquisition deliberately to create that inequality. *Punitive greed* is the same type of acquisition deliberately to leave the deprived suffering, powerless or disabled. Sometimes it takes fine grained analysis of circumstance and motive to distinguish these, but all the preceding involve overt behaviors, and the measure is the resulting inequities. Simple greed does not require intention, for instance while continuing to acquire in the face of others' deprivation a person denies greed explaining he is unaware of results; it is still greed, the measure being the resulting inequity. Next, passive hoarding which perpetuates extremes of inequity previously created is also greed. Next, greed is not always impulsive. It may be planned and calibrated; sustained effort and greed are not incompatible. Next, greed can be exhibited by person, group, corporation, even government. Common observation also shows personality differences. Not everybody exhibits the extremes of greed; but I believe all people act on the impulse at some time in their lives. Separately, greed can be purely mental, a longing, or craving, akin to obsession and addiction, not acted upon, but this is the province of the psychologist.

In practice, as James Childs points out, greedy individuals usually hoard both wealth and power (*31*).

The origins of greed are not mysterious. Like the origins of the drive for power the seeds are everywhere, and if a little bit feels good, more must be better. Previous lack is not necessary to start greed any more than fire is started by lack of fire, but like fire greed expands where it can, it has no internal homeostatic mechanism and the bigger it gets, the faster it grows. Its spread is also quickened by social imitation, akin to panic spreading through a crowd.

Greed is not a rational force.

As a concept greed has largely lost its moral sting. Few contemporary dictionaries include that it is reprehensible. The modern fashion not to sound judgmental, situation ethics, and the habit of social scientists to use past deprivation, social pressure, low self esteem, background, entitlement and myriad extenuating circumstances to explain the behavior, make the moral question so complex, all has crumbled into uncertainty.

This essay resurrects the moral dimension. If the consequences of greed are harm and pain, it is immoral. If greed is flaunted, when the pain is known, it is also sociopathic. These situations are quite common. Anyone doubting the concept of punitive greed should recall that the ancient book by Sun Tzu *The Art of War* is required reading in top corporate circles.

Not all wealth is created by greed, and not all inequalities are caused by greed, but if you could start with a society of complete equals, unrestrained greed will be sufficient to quickly render that society unequal.

It is also the purpose of this paper to suggest repairs, for which we need to know how our present problems started. Our founding economic theory is tangled.

You had to be Bold

The ordinary test of a philosophy is whether it makes people better and happier, whether it results in prosperity, cooperation and peace. Utilitarianism seemed a swaggering success because it dismantled the smothering pessimism of the Middle Ages, when a social caste system shackled your life chances, church dogma shrouded attitude and thought. Hobbes's dictum at the time was that life for Everyman was solitary, nasty, poor, brutish and short. Our current economic theory is based on a radically different idea.

You had to be bold bringing out new ideas in the European 1700s but they were revolutionary times and philosophers risked their necks pushing some new arguments that people were created equal and each had the liberty to create his own destiny. The French Revolution opened with its violence for equality. In England these ideas took shape as utilitarianism, a put-together philosophy that is neither profound nor poetic, but which was brazenly inclusive, and it confronted a national system of unbearably elaborate dogma and ancient ritual. Jeremy Bentham, Henry Sidgwick,. J.S. Mill and Adam Smith drew the footings.

Inverting the Problem

Rather than religious, utilitarianism uses secular, psychological motivators to explain human behavior, the emotions of pleasure (happiness) and pain. Pleasure is a good. Its ethics: units of pleasure and pain can be summed and compared, and we should choose the act that results in the greatest good for the greatest number, calculations that any person can do. Utilitarianism is practical, astonishingly democratic, and astonishingly rule-free. The utilitarians bluntly advised governments, let the people alone. Let them be human, doing what they do naturally.

So instead of having high priests and nobility dictating values, utilitarianism promotes the values of science, which are truth, practicality and factuality. Adam Smith's contribution was a step further, to give happiness a mercantile slant. In the new philosophy there is no conspicuous concern with sympathy, compassion, honesty, courage, grace, generosity, altruism, charity, beauty, purity, love, care nor honor. It accepts that humans are fundamentally selfish and egoistic and that they don't care about society-as-a-whole. So how does utilitarianism reconcile the selfishness of individuals with the common good—a problem no other social philosophy had solved? Adam Smith's breakthrough was inverting the problem. He simply declared that the selfishness of man and the good of society go together. The general welfare is best served by letting each person pursue his own interests. Each unit egoistically strives to better his own lot and maximize his own pleasures. In exerting himself so, he looks for efficiency, for better ways to make money. He'll invent a better way to cure hides or find a quicker delivery route, for entirely personal gain. But these are soundly rational moves from an economic point of view, and when everybody does this, it sums and spreads through the community, which is improved as if lifted by an invisible hand because no individual intended that end. And we note all of this is achieved without the value of justice, because justice, like the preceding list of noble values, is not a natural quality. It requires rules, and utilitarianism is fundamentally to be rule-free.

Its writers were bold. Utilitarianism pitched a very big tent. As far as theories go, it is fabulously inclusive, reaching down from intrahuman emotions all the way up to prescriptions for nations. For Smith, a country is its economics.

Exported raw to America, this principle spread like wildfire, melding with the American philosophy of Pragmatism. Old morality withered, except where it became an instrument of economic progress. Little of value existed outside of usefulness, and a means-to-ends consciousness became urgent. It also emerged in the national consciousness that this pursuit was unlimited—this was the spirit of freedom.

At the end of the 1800s, enormous business and enormous acquisition was understood as heroic. It still is. We still believe in the invisible hand, and that the outsize wealth of the topmost benefits all. These are the footings of our contemporary capitalistic society and our progress in national wealth has been the awe of other countries.

Lost in the Rout

The typical high school textbook teaches a skimmed version of Adam Smith's argument that as the rich get richer, it's good for everybody. Not until he gets to college does the student find complications in Smithian capitalism, such as the persistence of inequalities, and of poverty. If the student pursues the study of economics he will eventually read texts containing "Indifference Curves" which show the economy actually does better with social inequality *(32)*. The original ideal of equality is tainted, the pursuit of happiness is full of conditions.

Utilitarianism runs into trouble with some simple counterexamples.

If we should judge an act by what brings the greatest good to the greatest number (the 'hedonic calculus') then, for instance, in setting up a factory to make cheap clothes, the pain caused to employees doing tedious work for low wages is offset by the greater benefit to the greater number of customers who benefit from cheap clothes, and the factory is a good idea.

This example shows how the hedonic calculus is a sum of pleasure units weighed against units of pain. It is a simple additive economics, held to be rational. But in each example, there is no provision for the minority caught offside. Why don't we have public executions?—the pain to the victim would be more than offset by the summed satisfactions of all the spectators. A second counterexample, in different circumstances: suppose, on a battlefield, a hand grenade is tossed in on five soldiers in a trench. If one of them throws himself on it, saving the lives of the others, the hedonic calculus makes this a good act. But utilitarian ethics is also satisfied if one of the soldiers is pushed or ordered onto the grenade because four lives are still saved at the cost of one. Other philosophical systems would consider that an entirely different act. The usual explanation for these counterexamples is that utilitarianism includes an understanding that we are all enlightened people with civilized motives. Selfish, yes; competitive, yes. But we would never take pleasure from the suffering of another human, and we are not cruel—we are simply not that kind of people.

We are a species of competitives, and each person is inclined to do what benefits him and utilitarianism does not recognize greed nor avarice as moral wrongs. It regards self promotion as rational. It does not list equality as a social virtue. The problem is, utilitarianism is a philosophy with no ideals to offend anybody—just what works.

In the 1800s, through its industrial stage, Smithian economics consumed whole cities, and in the rout, gentlemanly civilities were lost. Some people got prodigiously wealthy, others suffered. But Darwinism was also rising and the robber-baron acquired allies among the Darwinists who held that inequality is an unavoidable fact of nature, so in capitalism's results, no guilt. It held, there are only the strong and the weak. Historically, it took more than a century after Adam Smith for the western democracies to question child labor. Until that time, the invisible hand justified the misery of legions of ragged and barefoot children whose lives were ruined in dank mills and deep mines, whose profits made Britain and America so powerful (33).

Squeezes

In fact there are many ways to crack Adam Smith's theory and John Nash's (34) famous mathematical rebuttal is only one.

An elementary rule of logic is that when there is a contradiction anywhere within a theorem, the whole theorem is false.

The center of Adam Smith economics is a paradox. It says, what's good for the selfish individual is also the common good. Secondly, it says, when you and I are in competition, what's good for me is also good for you. Those two by fiat.

Next paradox: utilitarianism does have an indirect gesture at equality. The notion is that when many units compete under the same rules of market exchange, the ever-circulating of goods and money keeps the whole system fluid; units are free to enter and exit this system at will. There is only one system, the free market, so we are all in the same boat, so we all must be the same. In practice, of course, history shows us a boat or ship of state with sweating galley rowers down on benches in the bilge, and with people up on deck all dressed in colorful finery, their faces upturned into the glorious sun. Yes, we are all in the same boat. And what is different is supposed to be the same.

The fourth self-contradiction is that free market capitalism is supposed to rectify past inequalities by allowing free competition, which is something that results in inequalities.

Further, Smith's system cannot be regulated at the extremes where self-interest becomes the greed of not-so-well intentioned entrepreneurs, profiteers in cartels, and of corners, squeezes, and monopoly makers. All of these also want wealth but they are for the common bad.

But here is the most obvious point. Try to fit greed into the hedonic calculus and watch the ethics. Greed is the outstanding moral wrong because it reverses the utilitarian ethic, with greatest happiness for the smallest number.

The most popular way to handle paradoxes are to ignore them, of course. They take thought, and I'll argue later this is discouraged by our culture of bombastically bright entertainment. Another way is to repair them with rationalizations. Historically, the contradiction between the Constitution's talk of happiness and justice, and what was visible to the naked eye, that most workers' lives were still nasty, brutish and short, was rationalized by saying actually pain and suffering are good because they goaded the poor into greater efforts, thus the economy is energized. And this rationalization thrives today.

Since the promise of upward mobility is axiomatic in Smithian economics, we should take a closer look. Present inequality is vast enough, the chances for the poor to work to close up the gap are long gone. Inequalities of this magnitude tend to become hereditary (35) and by and large, the descendants of the American poor will be poor. Upward mobility is a sacrosanct notion in Smithian economics, very widely held because the freedom to move up represents hope—in some people's minds, this freedom rebuts all criticism of the system. Let's measure this myth. While there is freedom to move up adjacent classes (a stock hand may rise to supermarket manager in a lifetime), the same freedom allows many people also to fall, which is called downward mobility, and which occurs in similar numbers. But the chances of a person born poor climbing all five classes into the top ("making it"), while occurring in a few widely publicized instances, are too small to constitute a real freedom. (Remembering that the top is an extremely thin, long tip to a pyramid (36), one sociologist puts the upper class at roughly 3 percent of the population. About.7.7% of that has moved in from below—a minute, and historically persistent, figure (37)). The argument that everyone is free to rise to the top is dismantled in most introductory sociology textbooks—although a student must usually wait until college to read this. But the trick of flaunting possibility to mask actual probability is not a casual device.

These paradoxes are no less nonsensical because they are cross-stitched into the writings of professional economists. Economists have been building on Adam Smith's examples of pin factories and canal barges for more than two hundred years. Our libraries contain shelf upon creaking shelf of intellectual embroidery around these basics. But the end result is that today all we have is a long, groping slavery to principles which don't work; can't work; because some of Adam Smith's axioms don't even rise to the level of common sense.

Mystique

A historical detail: one of the popular distractions of Smith's era was spiritualism. The vernacular was everywhere. Rawls has unearthed a minor book in utilitarianism, F.Y. Edgeworth's *Mathematical Psychics*. In that era, leisure time for the upper classes was spent at seances. Sidgwick was president of a Society for Psychical Research and actually conducted experiments to evoke mysterious forces. Science was in its infancy. And Smith's "invisible hand" is not a scientific principle. It is a mystical concept.

Marx's principles were once the major rebuttal, but now that communism has largely collapsed (of the world's 260 countries only 5 now are communist) Adam Smith's doctrine appears to emerge again, as if the winner, a victorious truth. If size is success, the showcase example is today's megacompany, the corporation "overweeningly powerful and accountable to no one" (38), almost magical, because the belief also lives that once a certain high level of anything is achieved, you are invulnerable and above the law. This is a place where heroes live—the Nietzschean mystique—where big things get done, where no one is slowed down by theoretical contradictions.

Money Happiness

Recently, psychologists have provided a decimating argument against Smithian theory. Ryan and Deci (39) have summarized a whole literature in psychology on the antecedents of human well-being. Psychologists have always wondered what makes people feel good, and for decades they have quizzed people on the intricacies of happiness. The general answer, all the more reliable because it is based on voluminous and cross cultural research, is that money is not a reliable route to happiness. Happiness is based on other, internal factors. The relation of wealth to well-being is tenuous; only below the poverty line does money bring well-being, above it, increases in personal wealth do not bring increased happiness. A corollary finding is that the more people focus on financial and materialistic goals, the lower their feeling of well-being. Finally, certain people tenaciously believe that money does bring happiness; they are the unhappy. Together, these findings largely dismantle Smithian theory of human motivation. For the present essay it also means that the motivation behind greed, pursuit of material wealth to extremes, cannot be for the happiness it brings. There is nothing heroic about greed. It is closer to obsession.

In fact, after the fall of communism, most of the original problems of industrial capitalism have reemerged too—in different guise. Instead of local factories and mills, we have transnational corporations, just as indifferently employing hordes of unprotected labor, including children, for egregiously low wages in foreign countries.

All notable developments for a philosophy that was invented against privilege and tyranny.

Making It

If we are to build up a system with paradoxes, we must promote contradiction as we go. This begins with the contradictory myths we are teaching our children.

We are currently teaching our young two incompatible morality tales.

Horatio Alger's children's books from the 1800s tell the story of a boy from ragged tenement origins who struggles from poverty up to riches in an urban odyssey of unflagging effort, single-minded ambition, determination, tenacity and hard work. The boy hero meets tyrannical employers, jealous competitors, wily criminals, prejudice and derision of the poor. He defeats mountainous odds to emerge finally on top, financially successful, pulling his own mother up out of poverty, and this all with his good character intact, in a world where the good guys always win.

The youngest minds get molded around the idea that this sort of ambition makes a person invincible. This myth instills a trust in long term, hard work.

Yet in the same semester our schoolchildren learn the opposite value: how to turn a quick profit using cunning and slick chatter. A contemporary of Alger's, Samuel Clemens (Mark Twain), wrote luminous country tales, regularly read to children. In one, Tom Sawyer, a juvenile in a mid-nineteenth century American small town, is ordered to complete a wearying chore one beautiful Saturday morning, to whitewash a long fence. But our Tom is a gifted talker, and he figures a way out of the task. As each of his friends comes walking by, Tom plays the work up to be a magically rare opportunity, and his friends, persuaded, compete for a chance to try it, actually paying Tom their toys to let them paint the fence. More friends come by and Tom gets rich from all their prize possessions while getting them to do the work for him until the task is done. The story is imagetic and funny, but it values slyness over effort, and it makes a clear point of getting ahead by exploiting one's friends. Despite the phosphorescent prose, this tale is about skimming and suckers in a world where the good guys do not win. In it, winners are people who subtly know how to manipulate the wants of others (*40*).

It would be nice if children generalized from Alger and colored themselves all industrious, righteous, honest, rational and forward thinking. But growing up, some of us have absorbed the point that hard work is for dupes, and that out of the sleeve of ambition comes the hand of greed.

Distraction

The topic of greed battles with a powerful distracter.

Poverty, I have argued, is partly a product of unfettered greed.

But since the 1970s we have been captured in the orbit of a certain kind of argument, that we have poverty and scarcity because our planet Earth has limits and we are running out of food and raw materials.

Actually there is a new consciousness on this point. Analysts Mark Sagoff [41] and Bjorn Lomborg [42] head this argument. Since the 1970s environmentalists have been predicting energy will be dangerously short because we consume too much. These predictions are framed in phrases of standard economic theory, in material terms, with mathematical projections of dire depletion and collapse of the ecosystem if we continue at present rates. They state we will imminently see starvation among industries for materials, accompanied by starvation among people.

But these predictions simply haven't turned out. Both analysts document that since the 1970s the world's most basic resources have actually become more abundant and cheaper. There are ultimate planetary limits, of course, but we are nowhere near. Malthusian arguments that starvation exists because there are 'too many people' don't compute. In far too many places where the absolute level of food supply is adequate, there is famine. The world now produces enough food for everyone to have an adequate protein-rich vegetarian diet if the food was equally distributed.

But, says Sagoff, neither technology nor economics can address the major causes of starvation which are corruption, mismanagement, ethnic antagonism, war, trade barriers, and social conflict. *Absolute levels of raw resources are not getting worse; what is getting worse is the difference in income between the wealthy and the poor.* Technological methods will not bring solutions. Not until we try a solution that turns on the moral will we begin to see improvement.

Scarcity is man made. The whole debate needs a new pivot.

There is a lot of misery worldwide, and the argument that there is abundance for all who would only try is false. We need a new paradigm to explain life-threatening scarcity in the face of plenty.

The Pivot

What drives this society? We proudly answer that what fuels people in this nation is a competitive drive to be better. The obvious result is inequality, because the intention is inequality. Competition deserves a closer look.

Anthropologist Ruth Benedict summarized her overseas work saying the most obvious difference among societies was whether the living was cooperative or competitive. This was the 1930s. She used the term synergy. A high synergy society is socially cohesive, cooperative and unaggressive—one person's acts at the same time serve his own advantage and that of the group, his gain results in a gain for all. But cultures with low synergy are highly competitive and the individual gains advantage only at the expense of another, aggression is prized, indeed humor originates from one person's victory and another's demolition. Low synergy eventually threatens the social fabric. Her example was the Dobu of New Guinea, whose daily atmosphere of ill will and treachery among all made it a showcase of Hobbesean nastiness, and feared among its neighboring tribes. The Dobu have no chiefs, no government, no legalities and live very close to the "state of nature" philosophers propose. Danger is at its height within the tribe, not from without, and the attitude lives that it is prudent and right to inflict pain on losers to protect your win. Hierarchy is based on ruthlessness which is admired, and inequality and injustice are believed to be in the nature of things (43).

Benedict pointed out the world's societies can be arranged on a continuum from those with the highest synergy to those with the lowest.

In our own society, we love competition and we promote inequality. A team of sociologists headed by C.S. Fisher (44) has recently tightened this argument with a treatise that first attacks the Bell Curve explanation that inherited differences in IQ and natural talent can be used to explain our unequal fortunes. They summarily deny the economist's claim that inequality fosters economic growth. Third, they state, our inequalities are by design, and they are growing. The result is that in the last twenty years we have become a steeply hierarchical society, and this is with popular support. We are choosing inequality through government economic policies that chronically distributed wealth unfairly.

Clearly our own society has lower synergy than we boast—and it's falling.

Simply, any free market culture that would rather create a market in a resource than have abundance for all is creating inequality as it goes. But so long as we can attribute unhappiness to global limits, or to inherited individual differences, then nature is to blame. We can hoist a paradox. We can both have our levels of misery and congratulate ourselves on our modern attitudes and on a humane society.

Manipulation of Hope

That last hypocrisy is researched by two Yale scholars, Guido Calabresi and Philip Bobbitt (45) who argue we practice inequality everywhere while pretending to equality (it is so close to our notion of justice). This subversion requires a nest of contradictory customs, a shell game designed to help us avoid and deny the moral consequences. And a retreat to other standards: sometimes, conceding inequalities, we will go through contortions to show that at least we are humane. The cost of all this, of course, is honesty.

Calabresi and Bobbitt argue that instead of universal abundance, there is perpetual scarcity. We calibrate it so. Society oscillates between two kinds of decisions. A first order decision is how much to produce or allow of a desirable good, and a second order decision is who shall get it. If this process were obvious, we would be outraged at the insight that there is needless suffering, because the scarcity is man made. Whether the desirable good is shelter, life-saving medical treatment, an education, or decent treatment by the police, we simultaneously manage the perception that all is well when in fact it is well with only a fraction of the population. Seeing certain medications or (in war) draft-deferments only go to the rich, or seeing that with our aggregate wealth, poverty need not exist, we search for reasons that suffering comes to some people but not others. The focus becomes methods of allocation. The central insight is to see that allocation by itself is an act signifying inequality. We realize certain methods of allocation are "acceptable," meaning they do not morally offend, for instance, the free market method acceptably allocates hunger because it decentralizes choice into individual decisions, and we can blame the hungry person. So this distracts from the scarcity itself. And hope is preserved. But each allocation method is rather arbitrary. We wonder if, keeping the same overall percentages, poverty could just as well be allocated by lottery. The market does not acceptably allocate the draft, so we have to shift to another method of allocating that inequality. Mistakes in choosing allocation method pull back the curtain on the fact of the original scarcities, creating fear and outrage. But the reality is, the scarcity of doctors, on whom lives depend, is a result of a human decision how many to train—and not a limitation of Earth's carrying capacity.

Sensation-hungry Press

While we are uncomfortable with the fact that the market runs an "acceptable" number of auto deaths, cancer fatalities, or hungry four-year-olds, it allows us to explain each case as personal misfortune. It will appear there is no other choice, and our morality is preserved.

So while we believe in a strong, happy society, brimming with progress and good for all its people, we get daily news hinting at our less-civilized status. The facts are, shelters for battered women are always crowded, fear permeates some schools, barbarism spreads in our prisons, and in some precincts it is becoming harder to distinguish police behavior from that of criminals. Calabresi and Bobbit continue this argument describing a societal device we use in huge efforts to preserve this contradiction.

The perception of humaneness is crucial. It tells us our system is both strong and good; otherwise glimpses of inhumanity are a dangerous hint that things are not working. Two examples: some years ago, a million dollars was spent on the rescue of a single downed balloonist in a dramatic, highly publicized race of helicopters and boats. The drama proved our humanity. We make massive efforts for someone in distress. What was never publicized was the chronic underbudgeting of the Coast Guard which otherwise would make such rescues routine. In a second example, heroic amounts were spent to rescue prisoners from a fire in a penitentiary. But what was never revealed is that the prison's scarce medical resources meant hundreds of others routinely went without treatment or died at other times. This type of rare and heavily publicized humane event, fed to a sensation-hungry press, creates a "sufficiency paradox", an "illusion of sufficiency" *(46)* that the goodness is there for us all. Generalized, this creates the illusion of abundance. The media deal in demonstrations of sudden and spectacular humanity. But for every person who gets the rare benefit, many others do not. A life-saving kidney goes to one of several people in need, and the life-taking decision about the others is not publicized. The "illusion of sufficiency" device massively confuses possibility with probability but on a societal level, it is a media-promoted and effective manipulation of hope.

We too use Potemkin villages.

Kafkaesque

What about all the people who lose to scarcity? People hate themselves for failing, but unless society is honest, they must absorb the original scarcity plus the anguish of not knowing how they failed and not knowing what to do. To the loser the frustration and humiliation of not knowing why, creates "the Kafkaesque cost of being in a process without knowing how to help oneself" *(47)*. If people compared our national inequities in wealth with the insight that, through decided levels of scarcity, the aggregate amount of suffering is controlled, public emotion could erupt.

Calabresi and Bobbitt's point is that we must keep examining our values. Equality and honesty are prime values. But in these machinations, they are chronically opposed. We must chose honesty, then we can begin the struggle to reclaim our real humanity.

Corporations

Next we bring into this mix the vastly wealthy American transnational corporation.

Businesses exist to make profit. Corporations are a type of business association, ones with special legal powers and durability. They have been a usual part of the business environment since the fifteenth century. International corporations were the muscle behind European colonization in the second half of the last millennium, but in that era of horse and sail, their power was a fraction of what it is today. Some corporations have now grown gigantic, actually becoming global forces with more power and resources than some countries.

Actually the largest corporations derive power not only from wealth but because they can fluidly migrate to whichever nation offers the least legal restraints, the cheapest labor, the most amenable economies and the friendliest politics. In this sense they float above the world's constraints.

But as a rule American corporations differ sharply from the nation which hosts them. They are alien to the notion of democratic responsiveness, internal or external. In the universe of corporations everything focuses on the acquisition of resources, labor, and markets. These are the sources of power. Inside corporations Equality hides her face.

Corporations are not elected, so they are concerned with nobody's approval. Aside from occasional shareholder meetings, they never ask the public for ideas or permission. Nor do the workers elect their leaders. Inside, most business corporations are steeply hierarchical structures, in which employees' freedom to do what they want is openly bought for the wage. They are not responsive to the will of those they employ; some have inner dynamics that are feudal; some of their hierarchies are also jungles of dysfunction. In democratic America most corporations are iridescent examples of autocracy, thriving on soil where the Constitution guarantees everybody's freedom and equality.

Nevertheless, the overwhelming portion of our population denies any problem. Charles Derber, among several writing on this topic, believes there are specific reasons we don't even think about corporations. First, we are all educated to look elsewhere, for instance to unchecked government, as the primary threat to freedom. Second corporations make and sell our creature comforts, so we can't tamper with them without threatening our prosperity. Third, we feel powerless. The concentration of corporate power is inverse to people's feelings of personal power. Fourth, we see no alternative (48).

Powers without Obligation

If wealth is the only standard we use to judge, then we have to admit corporations are staggering successes and everything to venerate. They absorb people's lives. We consume their products daily, use their services hourly, rely on them for information. We are dependent. We compete to work in them.

What protects them is that we are taught the system is rational. We are also taught that the goodness of a society depends on how well its topmost members are doing, so the higher our topmost members, the more they are discussed with awe.

The natural foe of corporations is government. But international corporations are so wealthy they slide over governments. They have become like tourists in their own country. As they lose national loyalties, they come close to becoming powers without obligation. As the largest transnational corporations grow, they become sovereign and untouchable (49).

The Corporate Personality

Roughly there are, I suppose, two kinds of people. The first divides the world into Good versus Bad. The second divides the world into the Strong versus Weak. These two types never can communicate. Among the latter, the concern is never to be caught weak because hell takes the hindmost, and among them all talk about goodness and ethics is irrelevant, and every effort is given to staying strong. This second type infests corporations. They are refractory to talk of humanity and you can shout all you want and they will not listen; every ounce of their attention is given to their competition.

Their rules of engagement are Darwinian.

Large scale competition among these massive corporations is what upgrades greed from whimsical excess to lethal force.

Two Areas of Corporate Control

First, Christopher Lasch points out that private universities depend on corporations, through investments, grants, or otherwise; and wherever their money is used, corporations influence state universities too. Consequently you will find free discussion on university campuses on almost any topic but one. Academic debate is not used to deconstruct the corporations that feed them.

The News

The second important area of control is corporation ownership of the media.

Through corporate competition, we now live in a system in which a few colossal media conglomerates dominate the news outlets. A typical conglomerate owns film studios, television studios, publishing houses, retail outlets, theaters, newspapers, music studios, cable channels, and in some cases, amusement parks. This oligopoly of conglomerates is small. It has overwhelming financial power, and it is not responsive to the will of the public.

Corporations exist for profit, so the news has become a commercial product. Largely, the same mentality making decisions about entertainment is now making news decisions (and the two, according to Neal Gabler, are increasingly difficult to tell apart $_{(50)}$).

Analyst Robert McChesney $_{(51)}$ says commercialization of the news has been a slowly growing process, starting in the 1840s when it was realized that selling news could actually make an entrepreneur money. Greed rather than journalistic standards took journalism astray in the era of the Yellow Press when stories were written for what sold and all the money came in from readers. Later on, newspaper owners started getting bigger money from advertisers. Nobody objected, because then as now, the myth is that the prime enemy of a free press was the government, that competitive free market capitalism would always keep the media unbiased and democratic.

Missing Topics

We do have some control over which media programs we watch. We still can choose among television channels, but the overwhelming majority of channels are commercial, and corporations exert fine-grained control over the consumer's viewing diet. And unlike Canada's and Britain's, America's noncommercial channels are not guaranteed by the government. They depend on grants, charity and viewer contributions. They cannot hope for the stability, size and power of their commercials rivals.

The result? Television news viewers are carpet-bombed with advertising. Advertisers actually survey for the kind of news that is interesting to the viewers who have money to buy products. Advertising firms are so influential that current journalism avoids antagonizing them and politicians avoid antagonizing them. McChesney says their control extends to blacking out certain topics. So while education, drug testing, gay rights, religion are mentioned on commercial television, other topics such as the representativeness of the media system are never aired. Social class issues are avoided. If we live in a society of inequality, then we can wonder, every time the television shows us the upper reaches of abundant success, which scenes of poverty have been excised. Programs about the poor are rare.

In effect, says McChesney, "media firms effectively write off the bottom 15-50 percent of society." *(52)*

All of which, he continues, is undermining democracy.

Among McChesney's remedies: first, make how the media are used a political issue. Second, a separate 1% tax on advertising would raise substantial revenues (he estimates $1.5 billion annually) which could be used to subsidize the non-profit media.

Advertising

We absorb from the television, and that is what advertisers want.

We take advertising seriously. Over a hundred billion dollars are spent annually on advertising. Its goal is to occupy the drive and psyche of the nation with wants, so that the nation will spend.

But the media are doing much more.

It is decided not to show on television the varieties of fear in our rooming houses and alleys where people live in the lowest reaches of poverty. It is decided not to show our hungry people living in tilting rural shacks. Nor the ranks of exhausted faces in city sweatshops. Lost, abject, hostile, desperate, these people's glances are pulled aside by complicit belief that failure is the lot of the damned. These people are quite available for filming and quite imageable. Instead, television is filled with cacophonous distraction.

Contradictions are withheld in the news. For instance, new technology is lionized in commercials. But technology itself is amoral. For example, it is also making torture easier. No one would mythologize the kind of free market where people made profits marketing whips and thumbscrews, but a recent Amnesty International investigation reports that currently more than fifty U.S. companies manufacture equipment like stun belts and shock batons designed specifically for use on humans (these devices inflict great pain but leave little physical evidence) *(53)*. Difficult topics encourage thought, and they take time away from commercials.

War on Logic

Somehow the painful gap that exists between poverty and abundance must be anesthetized. Television is the means. We stuff television reality in the gap. Twenty-four hours every day commercial television is an ongoing polychromatic display of games, short dramas with gunplay and florid sex, perpetually interrupted by iridescent advertisements. Television both provokes fear and promises ecstasy in ultra short attention spans. It feeds a national obsession with beauty, teasing with glossy bodies, glossy cars, luscious scenery.

What is shown in commercials is overflowing abundance, specifically in terms of climactic moments. Now a race is run and now a prize is taken; now a man works for all of a second and a half, then it's time for beers; now all the cooking has been done, and a sumptuous meal is ready (54). The troubling theme is that human effort is noisily trivialized in commercials. This is the narcotic. Television lathers a bright, noisy blur over anything like sustained effort, perseverance, focused long term goals, and over a society with chronic stresses.

The evening news systematically distorts normal time. Downtown riots in Seattle are given less than a minute (some of which is the reporter's talking face), shift to shots of a dog frolicking in a fountain, shift to minutes of a freeway chase. The picturesque is pursued, the serious is trivialized.

These are moves in a war against logic. And if you watch television, you are having your thinking disrupted. The busy-ness of rapid shifts of focus, the effervescent color, the edgy, dramatic music, all make it difficult for viewers to build independent ideas.

Neuroses

But instead of asking what the frenetic distraction is about, we follow suit, with impulse. It's not just that advertisers say, you can solve your problems by drinking our wines or wearing this underwear. It's not just that each product is introduced as if it was the future of mankind. It's that the commercial saturation has been effective. No one mentally argues with the advertising. The real loss is that advertising is now accepted as if it was information.

As with any other drug, we need increasing strengths. The only way to find out what television is doing to you after years of watching is to turn it off for a month. Turn it on again after abstinence, and it seems like a television's bid for our attention is like repeatedly shooting a pistol into a chandelier.

Television also grows neuroses in the corners of its watchers. It grows invidious comparisons in us. Comparison shopping, comparison socializing—eventually we live life by the method of comparisons. Television is carefully producing hordes of viewers who are good at one judgment, namely, whether the neighbor or the person sitting across the room is a little better or a little worse off. This powerful judgment, 'I'm a notch better than he; I'm not quite as attractive as she', is what Alfred Adler diagnosed as a neurotic style (55), with powerful motives to compensate. Television grows envy in us, and the fix is to acquire. The result is a powerful narcissism, and an increase in the rates of depression (56) among watchers who cannot keep up, unable to match their lives to television's perfection.

Greed, like many addictions, is all about the sudden and spectacular. Advertising is passionately decorative, if thin as a billboard. It serves the sudden and spectacular.

Against images of poverty, fear and hunger, television also churns routine optimism into its daily programming. All is delivered in a happy, chatty style. More, each day, television will be noisily emptied out and reinstalled the same.

Sum

In a free society, some people's greed inevitably means deprivation for others. This does not require environmental limits, it only requires persistent and competitive self-promotion, and in a vast nation whose economy is two hundred years devoted to these principles, we now inhabit a society with a small fraction of astronomically wealthy individuals towering over a growing mass in poverty. America is arguably now more unequal than any of the original European cultures, yet we cling to and proselytize a horribly outdated economic theory which implies equality but actually delivers more inequality. Greed is the outstanding wrong because it reverses the utilitarian ethic. It produces the greatest good for the smallest number. Democracy's founding virtues are freedom and equality, so greed without restraint, producing great inequalities, becomes an undemocratic force.

This is an amazingly complex economy but we still raise our young on sleeveless country myths. They never explain a market's preferences for ensured scarcities, designed inequalities, and increasingly segregated economic classes. Our schoolbooks teach, after the demise of communism, that there is no superior alternative to Smithian economics. Adherents believe that free market capitalism is the end of history.

Remedies

The reflexive defense, of course, is that we already have remedies. That we protect our poor with aid and support, that our government provides a safety net for the least fortunate in the form of welfare and food stamp programs.

These programs are a shambling failure. Reports detail the thin efforts of our sprawling agencies to get food to Americans who are now hungry. In California, of the millions who need aid, only 45% of the eligible are able to get food stamps even when they qualify. The other largest states show similar agency breakdowns. The hungry are trying other sources, so demand at food banks is rising (*57*). But Americans turning to emergency facilities are too often rebuffed. Cities are failing to meet an average of 26 percent of requests for emergency shelter, 30 percent of requests by homeless families. Government safety nets are simply broken, and at this writing some states are cutting back further (*58*).

We do not properly protect our poor. Decades-long efforts in the Great Society program and the War on Poverty have failed to improve opportunities for the poorest Americans. As an index of our current concern, consider the national allocation for Food Stamps. It stands at 0.0017 of the Federal Budget (*59*). Already tiny, Federal food assistance allocations actually declined from 1995 to 1999 (*60*).

I'll sketch other options that don't work.

What about private charity? Since droves of homeless people (one quarter of whom are children) still roam the big cities, since we have unfed hungry, and since it has been that way for a long time and is not getting better, private charity has obviously been ineffective. It is too little, or sporadic and unreliable.

What about the churches? Their purpose for existence includes helping the weak and needy. Curious for numbers, I divided the number of homeless (conservatively estimated at 700,000 on any given night, 2 million sometime during the year) by the number of Christian churches. This nation is filled with churches: the World Almanac lists over 330,000 Christian houses of worship (*61*). If each church took in 6 homeless, there would be no more homelessness. (We are taught that God and money don't mix. But actually the struggle between church and capitalism has always been subtle.)

What about positive thinking? With enough love and trust and hope and unity and sensitivity and inclusiveness, will antisocial greed disappear? Well, we might hope that goliath profiteering corporations will desist in their exploiting, voluntarily come to their knees and want to be part of godly world harmony. But they will not. Universal tolerance will not stop transnational corporations wringing their profit from the sweat of laborers' faces. And these bromides do not create change, just a lot of weary smiles from well wishers. On the topic of attitude, we'll treat smiling rationalizations the same, such as the rationalization that 'greed is the sin that's good for the economy'. This sort of solution is just a delay which will float us over relatively good times. At present we have relatively high employment, so the vast majority of Americans are at least earning some amounts of money. But this is like a tide risen high, which covers all manner of unsightly things on the sea floor. They are not gone. Should the tide go out, they will reappear. Opines business professor Jim Johnson, "If you ask where all this could be heading, in the event of an economic downturn, we could see another 1992 civil unrest." (62).

Stopping the Gap from Becoming Wider

Harvard's John Rawls (63) has a way to repair a whole society skewed into these inequalities. Rawls asserts the misery of some is simply not made acceptable by having a greater good, as proposed by utilitarianism, because that violates the principle of justice. First Rawls insists that in addition to freedom and equality, there must be a prior value in democracy, justice. And that economic rationality and justice should forever be opposed.

Rawls insists on a shift in focus. We should not judge a culture by how its topmost members are doing, but by how it treats its lowest. His solutions follow. First, this society should decide how low any member can go. That establishes minimum rights. It requires we identify the least-advantaged person in society, and draw focus to him. Next, the very top and the very bottom of society should be (and all intermediate levels should be) connected, as if by a loose linked chain. Then if the top rises, it pulls the bottom up with it. If the bottom moves up, that closes the gap toward equality. This arrangement does not prevent any upward rise; but it establishes consequences on movements at the top.

Other Remedies

We must look down. Even *Business Week* pointed out that if the current wave of prosperity recedes, America's many social ills, with hunger and homelessness, could return with a vengeance, editorializing that the Federal Reserve and Congress should be guided in their policy actions by what's happening at the bottom of society, not by the bubble at the top (64).

The mystique of poverty has to be cracked. A television series 'Lifestyles of the Broken and Hungry' would not top the popularity charts, but my point is that if media paid attention to the bottom rungs with one-tenth the insistence in our commercial advertising, remedial changes would occur. Further, public service messages resurrecting the concept of the common good, would be a beginning.

Actually remedies for greed do not have to be expensive, nor big, organized programs. Primary education depends on the skills of individual teachers, and if talented educators can reinstall the Golden Rule (Do as you would be done by) in their primary classrooms, some of the damage could be reversed. We need preventatives. Greed has to be reinstalled as a moral wrong, and in religious circles, as a sin.

Up the educational ladder, remedies will be resisted. Here lives the fashion for nonjudgmentalism. An extension of moral relativism, this trend to universal acceptance is a couple of decades old and "Who am I to judge?" is now the standard of the gentle classes and educated elite, even spreading to exotic healing practices and 12-Step programs where it is thought that to suspend judgment of self and others is for the betterment of society. This is nonsense. Comfort only brings inaction, nonjudgmentalism is moral vacuum (65), and eventually we will have no conscience to stop what is happening.

High on the academic ladder, of course, is economics but our best economic theory has delivered us contradictions and reverses. Volumes produced by economists, all written with graphite dispassion, seem to promote opposites, and you wonder if a coup was carried out by those adept at complicated thought. Just drive through any big city, you will see newsstands sporting magazines with glossy coverage of billionaires, these newsstands adjacent to people living among girders and sewage drains, alleys, scaffoldings and grates.

Among the social sciences, psychology may provide a specific remedy. *The Diagnostic and Statistical Manual of Mental Disorders* (*DSM IV*) (66) is a standard used by all psychotherapists. It is a compendium of all mental illnesses and it is used as a diagnostic tool in training psychiatrists, clinical psychologists and social workers. This book has been expanding through succeeding editions as more and more mental conditions have been described (which has expanded the domain of clinicians so far it is now said that about half America's population could be diagnosed with some mental pathology or other (67)). It is time that *greed* be listed in *DSM IV*. With well directed psychological research of course greed will turn out to be a personality trait with a distribution in the population, and personality tests will be able to screen for extremes.

Moral Inertia

So there is a moral cause here. But the average person hangs back from active protest.

The problem is, even if we are not personally greedy, we have connections to corporations that are. We are happy consumers. Challenging the company we work for—would that be hypocrisy? Second, activism, we think, is radical action, and what about all that street rant "if you're not with us, you're against us!"—but we cannot rebel because our corporation is also our rent, and we enjoy the good living we make, and we're not giving that up.

Perhaps that explains why our most articulate writers are so quiet on this topic. They also look within. So, bluntly, we need a whole new strategy for change, in which a person who feels he is part of the problem may also be part of the solution.

Enter some new thinking. Max Bruinsma is a sharp critic of the damage wrought by contemporary advertising in the service of relentless acquisition. But times have changed, he says, and he argues the polarizing slogans of past social revolutions (you're either with us or against us) don't apply. We're in a historical shift. The modern activist is different. The rationale: culture today is driven by commercial advertising. In it, a particularly worrisome new trend is for advertisers to soften up our thinking with billboard-size paradoxes. Building-size ads fill our view and state that buying a very mainstream computer (Mac) is 'thinking different'. Across the street another billboard shouts that acquiring a glossy SUV is a singular act of rebellion. Bruinsma quotes more examples: "Sometimes you gotta break the rules," (Burger King), "Innovate, don't imitate" (Hugo Boss), "Be an original" (Chesterfield cigarettes). The central insistence of these is that conforming = rebelling. And we remember the Orwellian slogans, Peace = War, Slavery = Freedom which, in *1984,* reduced a future society's minds to value-free mush.

Well, we can follow suit. We can generate our own examples of contradictions. So, perhaps, commercial success and social responsibility are not incompatible anymore. Everything is possible if you use self-contradiction; you are able to both work for a company, and rebel against it. Corporate rebellion = loyalty.

This leads to a technique a 'Sixties activist, Rudy Dutschke, once called "the long march through the institutions." It is a long term and less bloody strategy. Go in, behave—and take over. The new culture agent is stylishly dressed, well paid, and works in an plush ad agency, designing resplendent ads which promote the return to honesty and social justice, humaneness, equity and the common good (68).

The next revolution will be inside corporations.

Conclusions

As the rich get richer and the poor get poorer we drop our pretenses to humanitarian democracy, instead salute material excess, accept Darwinian business ethics, and pin up as our national polestar the most powerful corporations.

Money and effort maintains a particular way of seeing and evaluating our society; we focus on the topmost members, cover current inequalities with a rotating blur of nearly a trillion dollars of advertising a year, and by not paying attention to the lowest, we deny them. But they are there. Inevitably, as our economic tree reaches up, its roots grow further down.

It is not enough to say hopefully we accumulate layers of experience from error and progress. Technology will not deliver us equity. Logic has not delivered us equity.

We want our morality back.

Nuts

For readers thinking these themes overwrought, I'll describe a small game in which you can watch greed in the person sitting next to you. Three people sit around a kitchen bowl. You, the fourth person, with a timer, start off placing ten small items in the bowl—quarters, dollar bills, or nuts. Tell the three players the goal is for each of them to get as many items as they can. Tell them one other thing before they start: every ten seconds (you have your watch ready) you will look in the bowl, and double the number of items remaining there, by replenishing from an outside source (a separate pile of quarters on the side).

In the original Nuts Game, I used hardware nuts, and the players were college students. You would think the players would figure out that if they all waited, and didn't take anything out of the bowl for a while, then the contents of the bowl would soon get very big, automatically doubling every ten seconds. Eventually they could each divide up a pot that had grown large. But in fact, sixty percent of these groups never make it to the first 10-second replenishment cycle. They each grabbed all they could as soon as they could, leaving nothing in the bowl to be doubled, and each player wound up with none or a few items. This can be an energetic game. I've seen the bowl knocked to the floor and I've seen broken fingernails in the greedy melee. In the original game, players are not allowed to talk. Even when they are allowed to talk, not all groups collaboratively work out a patient, conserve-as-you-go playing style, necessary for eventual big scores. They don't trust each other.

This makes a good classroom demonstration of what greed can do. Actually mathematicians have designed a variety of these games, microcosms of the free economic process (69). Behind them all is a problem always nagging at Adam Smith economics. In the short run, what is good for the individual is bad for the group. The game is a microcosm of a community sharing a slowly regenerating resource (clean water, timber, whales) and individual greed can actually destroy the common good. The game involves two opposing rationalities: what is rational for the individual vs. what is rational for the group. And the resolution has less to do with reason than building a shared morality.

GREED II

◆

Is exploitation wrong?

This is not the first time the nation has produced dramatic economic inequalities. What are very wealthy people like? The everyday world of work vs. values of democracy. How assumption of self-interest leads to fear in the workplace. Freedom, the illusion of freedom, coercion. Exploitation. Credit cards. Meritocracy. Sociopaths. Corporations and the economic justification for the damage they do. Historically we are emerging from an era with no clear ideology, but an era in which materialism and business has expanded powerfully and internationally, and out of the vacuum two old, discredited ideologies, laissez-faire and Social Darwinism appear to be rising again in modern guise. These ideologies are still flawed; the first (contained in modern Libertarianism) vigorously promotes freedom but ignores justice and is indifferent toward democracy. The second is supported by science, is disinterested in humane values and accommodates exploitation as part of the nature of things. The search for a modern economic theory closer to reality. Is this a society of individuals rationally maximizing happinesses? Andrews's view: at least among the disadvantaged, it is a political economy of hope and fear. Remedies. (1)

Looking for morning news, I click on my computer. My internet provider flashes with color, the biggest houses, the biggest jewelry, the most expensive toys.

The internet's financial press waxes muscular—the economy's on fire!

Television is the same. The media are a river of adulation for all this glitter and the people who own it.

School textbooks carry a similar message. The economy is ever expanding, its power is unparalleled, we are now spreading free market capitalism around the globe, bringing unimaginable wealth and improvement to mud-level nations and countries sucked out by socialism, raising everybody, because that's what capitalism does.

Has everybody been raised here? Actually, with talk of equality written into this nation's founding papers, the scenery never looks right. The contrast between rich and poor grows, and this year has been no exception. As an acquaintance on the street puts it: every year there are more homeless people and every year the limousines get longer.

If the stated goal of the system was to gradually create inequality, it might also claim success.

We barely notice because we are adjusted. But if you are a foreign visitor, how does this nation show? A svelte Scottsdale, of course. Disneyland, of course. The flamboyant homes of the film stars. Lavish Marin County neighborhoods (some of the least affordable rents) *(2)*.

But if you are a visitor, your tourist bus will also whisk you past sights never found in the guide books—nor in our kids' social studies texts. Neighborhoods awash in shootings (1,200 gun injuries in South Los Angeles alone last year *(3)*), square miles of city filled with houses with barred windows, chaotic schools, downtown blocks of sweatshops, whole neighborhoods sunk in semi-literacy, drugs, gangs, fear and nightmarish jails *(4)*. Not everybody looks like they have been raised.

Imbalance

The numbers show a radically skewed society. Rather than pages of numbing statistics I'll sketch a couple of facts, the first from sociologist Steven Rose. If you drew a line on a building three stories high to represent the distance between the lowest and the highest family income, the average (median) income sits at only 10.5 inches off the ground and half the nation is clumped below that *(5)*. Second, despite the prodigious numbers of poor, housing for them is so scarce that of the 3,141 counties in the United States, in only 4 can a person making minimum wage afford a one-bedroom apartment *(6)*.

I believe this imbalance mauls the national psyche because the media repeatedly show us images of people and places from the beautiful upper stretches of that vertical line. In the comparison, thrown at us daily, most of us lose.

This nation equates decency with wealth and indecency with poverty. These media images also create floods of anxiety. Being "less than", being poor, carries a stigma. Another sociologist thinks we are so materialistic poverty now actually carries the shame that cowardice carried in earlier, warrior times *(7)*.

Tinkering

And actually if the economy is on fire, we have some funny facts.

The dollar has dropped to a fraction of what it was worth thirty years ago. No amount of policy tinkering has been able to stop manufacturing's chronic decline. The national trade deficit is at an all time high (meaning roughly, if it's foreign made we want to own it). Personal debt has reached swaggering amounts. And bankruptcies have ballooned, now running 1.46 million a year *(8)*, outstripping the divorce rate, also outstripping college graduations *(9)*.

Envy

Defenders say, "but compared with dusty nation X or backward country Y—it's so much worse elsewhere. We are the envy of the world."

When we compare nations, we should keep in mind who we are comparing. Every third world nation has a middle class, no matter how small, with houses, and those folks are still better off than our hordes of homeless. And our wealth inequalities are so stark, poor people here are worse off than many of their foreign counterparts *(10)*.

And if you start comparing nations, what about the quality of life? Are our 30 million citizens on antidepressants also the envy of the world? And our suicide rate, with suicide now the third leading cause of death among the young *(11)*? Here lurks the question of how much life is worth living.

Curtain

I wish I could get away from these inequalities, but I cannot. Fly away from it all? Board a plane, and we take off. Having settled in at cruising altitude on a flight, surrounded by other passengers, I look out the sun filled window and we float among the iridescent clouds and for a moment it seems we are transcending the world's concerns. Then the stewardess carefully draws the cabin curtain across the aisle between us and the passengers in first class section. This act is noiseless and delicate. All passengers' eyes are riveted on it.

Revolt

Nowadays, nobody seriously criticizes the rich. Criticizing the rich doesn't make much sense if you think you're going be one. But it wasn't always that way.

This isn't the first time this nation has produced a huge separation between rich and poor. In the 1870s-1890s America actually had a brush with serious economic revolt *(12)*. The trouble was started by common farmers in the hinterland—stake holders in the new frontier—dismayed that all their hard work didn't deliver.

The Civil War's aftermath was a time of immense capital growth for some and hopeless drudgery for others. Chicago and New York contained both wealth-aristocrats in frivolously decorated mansions that mocked European aristocratic manors, and on the other side, smoke-stained factories with legions of ragged workers. In the rural South rich plantation owners lived in white-columned country homes while paying barefoot field workers scrip they could only spend at the owner's store—contract labor working in endless debt. This was the era of flamboyant corporation owners in top hats chomping on outsize cigars, also the era of steep child mortality rates, pestilences that swept the streets, misery and short life expectancies for the poor.

It was an era of unrestrained markets, the era of monopolists who collaborated with each other in setting prices; little was illegal.

Following the Civil War, there were a couple of different currencies in circulation, one sinking in value and less reliable.

City banks peddled mortgages widely on new farmland they had never seen. A new farmer could be sign on in either currency. Then a national money contraction occurred, consolidating the two issues. Farmers took the fall. They were left owing the banks up to twice what they had signed for. Believing in the national promise that hard work brings wealth, they found they only worked and lost money on their slow-producing farms, then worked harder and lost more. Meanwhile, the banks flourished. They grew spectacularly. They argued they were only being patriotic.

Bewildered, farmers actually started trying to understand what was wrong by reading books on economics. The result was a bitter understanding of 'the money power,' of lenders rights, of monopolistic control, and of American credit corporations as fortresses of wealth.

In desperation, farmers' cooperatives started up. They aimed for debtors' independence. They were made up of plain people, seeking self expression. First in the South, this movement swept across Texas, then the Western plains states, attracting farmers by the thousand. Then they joined up with railroad workers who were desperate over low wages and ruinous equipment and were striking. Eventually the National Farmers Alliance and Industrial Union spread far west and north, and at its peak had over a million members. The Populist Party was started. This new party was virulently anti-monopoly, and its hero was the opposite, the poor-but-good worker. It successfully ran candidates for local government, and then William Jennings Bryan, a Populist, actually won the Democratic nomination for President. Bryan had risen from stump-speeches in open fields to the political crest with firebrand oratory telling farmers and workers they were "crucified on a cross of gold," nailed to the impossible demands of credit merchants, and the victims of a monied tyranny *(13)*.

The poor have always been demonized. But for the first time, in the 1890s, the rich were being demonized.

Bryan lost the election to McKinley in 1896. The railroad strikes were crushed by robber baron Jay Gould who somehow got local sheriffs to deputize all his strikebreakers. Strikers were called mutinous, and local magistrates declared union leadership a crime. Without Bryan rising, the Populist movement suddenly faded. There was capitulation and disgust. People muttered 'you can't fight the nation's banks.' Some farmers even left the country and moved to Canada. Corporate power rose everywhere again. Sentiment changed. In memory, words like 'the people's', and 'progressive', became tainted with the shadow of socialism.

That era is remembered in history books. But it has been so diluted that Populism is described as an agrarian movement, a protest. Omitted are the rage, the oratory, the fires, the marches, the riots, the militia shooting strikers.

I believe some of the early conditions of that movement are reappearing. But today we are mute. We are back to the dogma that whatever the wealthy do is good for the poor. Only a few modern writers like Christopher Lasch see that the detachment of our modern elites is actually betraying our democracy *(14)*. Fewer writers, like Charles Derber, are saying the moral decay in this country starts at the top *(15)*.

Atomized

We live in a peculiar era. There is said to be no ideology.

What is ideology? It is a visionary assertion of values, goals and aims. It ties a people together, explaining what is bigger and more important than each of us. It is part theory, part speculation. It urges loyalty. Ideologies can be national, grand and visionary, or subdued and local. They may be delivered from the podium, or they may be unspoken but lurking everywhere as if a colorless odorless gas that saturates a culture's thinking *(16)*. An ideology can move a community to prepare for war, or it can move a nation to peace; but it gives motivation and meaning, it states the common good, and explains why the people must work together. Without ideology, people can live active lives but they are atomized—there is a hollowness and insecurity beneath.

Daniel Bell wrote a book *The End of Ideology* which says that in the United States, ideology has dissolved *(17)*.

Bell: Through the last century—at least through the belligerent period of the two World Wars and the 1950s Cold War—the United States had plenty to say about what it stood for, also what it hated. Ideology was sharp and it was national. But with the advent of peace, and especially with decline of communism, there was suddenly less reason to deliver thunderous speeches about why we are here, what we are ready to die for—the speeches that bring urgency and purpose and meaning to people.

We have drifted since the Vietnam era without an ideological rudder. We exist in a kind of void, in which individualism flourishes, and narcissism, ego, materialism, the pursuit of self, wealth, status and greed. But nothing that moves the masses together.

Creeping

Predicting the future may best be left to crystal-gazers, but we can always take hints from newly published books because they contain ideas that may be influential for years.

Some new publications are unsettling. Into this void, I'll argue, are creeping two quasi-ideologies. Actually they are not new. They are two old ideologies, mutated, which are rising again.

First a popular book which appeared in 2002. It describes a part of this society. The way the author works is a new fashion and it is revealing.

Beyond that Curtain

Very rich people are hidden from us because they want it that way.

Naturalist Richard Conniff uses sociobiology to describe the upper class. He has patiently followed the superrich around (and these folks are above 'junior wealth' which is about $5-10 million) and has interviewed them in their natural environment.

This is the new fashion, to explain what humans do because of their genes and their evolution. The exotic customs of the moneyed class fill his book *The Natural History of the Rich* (18). Because he is a naturalist he unflinchingly compares the people at the top with the alphas (top members) of other animal species.

Conniff says the superrich are an intensely narcissistic and competitive small group. They arrange their lives so that wherever they go (Aspen, Monaco, Paris) they see the same few hundred people. They are self-encapsulated. They regard the rest of us as "irrelevant, uninformed, even subhuman." and they don't like to talk to us. (One fabulously wealthy lady used her cell phone to call her chief-of-staff who was in another country to call her maid to tell the maid what to do next. The maid had a cell phone and was on the opposite side of the room from the lady).

Conniff reports that just like other top animals, the superrich are driven by the quest for status, mating opportunities and dominance, except that the human version constantly denies it.

Waste to Impress

Top-rungers also flout the basic rules of economics. While average folks purchase more stuff when it becomes less expensive (supply and demand), the leisure class prefers to buy stuff that is more expensive, even when comparable stuff is available for less. The object is to dazzle. Sociologist Thorstein Veblen identified that odd habit back in 1899 and termed it 'conspicuous consumption.' It's waste in order to impress [19, 20]. Conniff points out animals do this too. The cascading tail feathers of alpha male peacocks have no useful function. They are there to impress other peacocks—in fact they are so conspicuous they practically prevent the bird from flying.

More biology: the way the superrich have isolated themselves for centuries now qualifies them as a "pseudospecies". By hanging out and mating only with their own kind, over many generations, they have effectively removed themselves from the gene pool.

Top Baboon

Sociobiology is a fairly new division of biology. It's been around since the 1970s. It holds that human behavior is genetically shaped, like animals which run largely on instinct. It says our behavior is evolved. Sociobiology has a younger sister, evolutionary psychology, which talks more about humans than animals, but in the same way. Evolutionary psychology holds that our daily routines and our choices are not nearly as spontaneous as we think because our behavior and our emotions are determined by the long tracks of natural selection. Both these disciplines are in their infancy. Both are busily looking for parallels between animal behavior and our behavior to show we are more instinct than we think.

So what Conniff does is to illustrate the dominant posturing of top rats versus the belly-crawling of their subordinates, and the bluster of top baboons versus the rump-presenting submissiveness of subordinates—and compares it to the obsequious behavior of human underlings who attend to our superrich. Dominance patterns in this species fit dominance patterns in that. So for instance in both human and walrus communities, the top elite have more. They copulate more, they get more of what they want, and they guard more resources than they need.

Conniff states: "Humans seem to be 'ethologically despotic,' like chimpanzees; that is, we have a natural predisposition to hammering other people into submission." Except that in human males this is expressed as a "single-minded determination to impose their vision on the world" (21).

Hierarchy

Why do the rest of us go along with this? We can't help it. A stare from high authority throws us into rabbit-panic. Lower ranking humans throw themselves into submission, even sacrificing themselves for their high superiors. It's all biologically evolved behavior.

Inequality is everywhere in the animal kingdom. Even animals that can't do much else, such as chickens, are expert at knowing the ranks of all other chickens. And a low ranking wolf will fight to the death for its pack even while its daily life is made miserable by cruel tormenting from the animals above it because belonging to a hierarchy is everything. According to sociobiologists, hierarchy chains us too. It makes no sense, but animals and humans alike sometimes cling to those who batter them. It's in the genes.

Mayhem

Along the way, it would be heartening to learn from sociobiologists that our top people are good people. That part is missing. The ultra rich are likely to have serious mayhem in the family history. Conniff traces this old saying to Balzac: 'Behind every fortune there's an undiscovered crime.' Generations ago, many alpha families originally ascended by force and illegal conquest—and, in his interviews, often show themselves proud of it.

And what of our popular belief the wealthy are that way because they work very hard? Do they? Well, maybe. Conniff interviewed one extremely wealthy woman who told him, "I'm the most normal, normal person, I'm not like most rich people. I work really hard. Most rich people I know don't do anything but eat, drink, sleep, pardon the term, fuck, and have a good time" (22).

Genius and Alcoholism

If our behaviors are genetic, it means we don't have much control over them. Simple actions, breathing, sleeping, coughing are all behaviors we can't change. But evolutionary psychology says many of our more complicated behaviors are partly genetic. We have a 'genetic predisposition' towards overeating or dominance or addiction or depression, musical genius, alcoholism, and possibly some criminal behaviors too—because these things have been found to run in families. Today's cutting edge research is looking for behaviors that are controlled by genes, and how much. There is a scale called a 'heritability index' that runs from 0.0 to 1.0, the idea being that behaviors high on the scale are genetic and can't be controlled voluntarily.

Treacherous

The implications ripple across our legal system. If it was established that somebody has a genetic disposition towards criminal behavior, then he doesn't have control over it. Think of the possibilities: imagine a criminal lawyer putting on the following defense, "...Your Honor my client is not to blame—he couldn't control his thieving—he was just fulfilling his genetic destiny..." In fact these legal defenses may become more common as evolutionary psychologist are now arguing that using pornography *(23)*, not paying child support *(24)* and rape *(25)* are in the genes.

Evolutionary psychology is deliberately pushing into public policy. The appearance of a new book *Evolutionary psychology, Public Policy and Personal Decisions* shows its intended scope *(26)*.

Selfish

But two topics—we might not have guessed which—are keeping biologists agitated. Are we run by selfishness? And how important is the individual, as opposed to the group?

This is the way it's coming down:

1. Selfishness. Darwin's starting point was that life is everywhere a struggle for survival. If you want to survive, you can't waste time helping others. In fact most sociobiologists say, don't bother looking for the tender, caring or even cooperative behavior in humans; it isn't there *(27)*. But the central issue being kicked around: is selfishness by itself sufficient to keep a group surviving? Or does also a species of animals also need another type of behavior, like cooperation or altruism, in which members help each other? One camp, the hard-nosed Darwinists, says yes to selfishness—that also means genes-powered greed, genes-powered waste-to-impress *(28)*—and no to altruism.

2. Selection between whole groups. Darwin said natural selection happens between individuals. But what about selection between communities (and herds and flocks)? This issue is so hot, arguments between sober academics almost read like kids having tantrums. The point is this: if there is competition between groups (communities) for survival, the winning group will be stronger because of

teamwork, which takes something like cooperation or altruism between members. A group of only selfish individuals is weakened from within.

And these two issues go hand-in-hand. Orthodox Darwinists say, you don't need to think about altruism because there is no group-level selection.

Bogeyman

Daniel Batson writes on this debate. At this point sociobiology is new, and unsure. It keeps issuing statements then correcting itself. Does natural selection exclude group selection? Yes; correct that, no. Does natural selection produce only selfishness? Yes; correct that, no (29). Actually this is not just a scuffle under the stairs between academics. Because of Darwin's assumptions, all this threatens the very planks on which the theory of evolution rests. So a lot of people are watching this fight (30).

When these infant disciplines finally get their sea legs, they will bring home the bogeyman of all questions, because selfishness and altruism are not just behaviors, they are moral values. What's really lurking behind this work: is our morality controlled by our genes? (31).

And who Cares?

Adam Smith cares. Recall that Adam Smith's *Wealth of Nations* tells us, all people act in their own interest (selfishly)—and that is fine, according to him because the whole community eventually benefits. Who does this sound like? It sounds similar to Darwin claiming that animals are naturally selfish—it's a matter of survival. Both Smith, in *Wealth of Nations,* and Darwin don't truck with altruism. It would change the basic assumptions of both their whole theories. And we get the hint that Charles Darwin and Adam Smith were singing off the same sheet of music.

Social Darwinism

So the appearance of Conniff's book waves a flag. Any alliance between biology and big money should keep us nervous. This alliance has a scurrilous history.

A contemporary of Darwin's was English philosopher Herbert Spencer. Spencer was not only thinking on the same tracks, it was Spencer who invented the term "survival of the fittest." Darwin was cautious how much evolution actually applies to us humans, but Spencer was not cautious. Spencer applied "the fittest" to the wealthy (32).

Spencer became very popular with the monied classes towards the end of the nineteen century. On the lecture circuit here he said humans, like the animals described by Darwin, are all in a competition for survival. This was normal. For wealthy industrialists to exploit and discard hordes of poor in their factories was also understandable. The poor were the unfit. Nature was 'red in tooth and claw.' The industrialist was just hastening nature's way of weeding out the weak members. Spencer also said welfare, even charity, was a bad idea. It encouraged the poor, who would multiply and spread their unfitness. Overall, did the rich prosper at the expense of the poor? Of course—and in the long run, Spencer said, this was good for a nation.

After World War I, Social Darwinism was discredited as a vulgarized version of Darwinism. At the time communist ideology was flourishing in Europe, and the argument that the workers were going to control everything was turning Russia inside out like a glove. Socialism was on the rise in Europe, and America decided to keep one eye on its poor. Pro-worker feeling grew and between the World Wars, President Roosevelt built a more poor-friendly, worker-friendly atmosphere, and started Social Security.

But it is now sixty years since World War II, and times have changed again.

Won't Sit Down

During this last century, of course, many things changed. Science itself made vast progress, reaching peaks, so that at 2000 it could point back at a moon walk, the atom opened, the defeat of plagues as points on its startling ascent.

Today science has tectonic credibility. It is unimpeachable. If a layman attacks science, nobody listens.

But this topic, Darwinism, will not sit down.

Among the few with credibility to question science are philosophers. Philosophers are carefully trained in logic.

Con

Philosopher Richard Perry, in the staid journal *Ethics*, quietly walks up and kicks the struts out from under sociobiology.

Is it really science? Or is it a con?

Perry shows the logic under all sociobiology to be not the grid of deductive logic you would expect in science, but only a patchwork of analogies.

Now there is a certain use for analogies, but analogies do not prove anything, they only show likenesses. The best use of analogies is in the persuasive arts, oratory and poetry.

Analogy is the warp-and-woof of sociobiology. That's what they do, says Perry. If you want to say humans are aggressive, describe the aggressiveness in rats—show the similarities. If you want to prove humans territorial, talk about the territoriality of mockingbirds—invite the similarities. And so on.

Perry says, but wait. Why these analogies in the first place? There's something odd about circling around one species to make pronouncements about another. Why are we studying animals to understand humans? Would you investigate houseflies by studying blue herons? Wouldn't that distort what we already know about flies?

His article "Sociobiology: Science in the service of ideology" warns us the logic is so bad, sociobiology should be embarrassed. It is more like weaving a net with the study of animals and throwing it over humans. And it should tip us off to ulterior purposes. We should look for what else it does.

Perry urges us to decline trust in sociobiology. It is engaging reading. But it does what Herbert Spencer did. It tells us we don't have to feel guilty if we are brutal with each other—animals do it. It gives comfort to perpetrators of social injustice *(33)*.

Slave-making Ants

The next point in this essay is that Social Darwinism, or some modernized variation, is rising again.

Supported as a science, our neo-Darwinism is fed by hours of exquisite photography on Discovery Channel where we repeatedly watch hungry leopards stalk innocent deer, fell them and gorge on their entrails hour after hour. (What car salesman hasn't watched, and said to himself, that animal lives in me, I can use any method to drag down fleeing customers?)

Darwinism has a dangerous ally. Another twist in logic which always gatecrashes the party and says, if it happens in nature, it must right.

But the problem is, *you cannot logically convert a fact into a right*. (Example: it's a fact some kids beat up other kids on the playground, therefore they have a right to do it).

Morality should step in.

It took a long time to get that right, in western civilization. Because it's a fact Charles Darwin reported on a species of slave-making ants, humans do not have a right to make slaves.

Then as now, using analogy as a justification for ignoring human pain and fear, or creating it, is a perversion.

Place your Bets

Social Darwinism will be much harder to get rid of this time. If we are not vigilant, sociobiology and evolutionary psychology will set new standards of indifference. The implications are stirring. What if our politicians and policy makers, administrative agencies and bureaucracies, our military, our justice, our legislators, watching, all believe that rich and poor, good and bad, winning and losing are in the genes? Place your bets, because depending on the way a couple of these controversies turn out (especially selfishness) we may have biologists telling us what is right and wrong, that democracy is unnatural, and that inequality and injustice are in the nature of things.

Laissez-faire

Laissez-faire was the table-thumping cry of monopolistic big business in the 1860s through the 1920s—overlapping the Populist era, but on the capitalist side. From the businessman's point of view, this was the Gilded Age. Will power was a virtue, expansion always seemed the way to go and everything was believed to be better if it was bigger. (The Crystal Palace, the Eiffel tower, and the Titanic were industrial symbols). The concept traces back to 1825, and it means government abstention from interference with individual action, especially commercial action.

But it was found that if business was not restrained at all, the economy rose and fell in a destructive cycle of peaks and crashes. Second, it produced monsters that worked people to disease or death. During the *laissez-faire* era people died or got maimed on the job in perilous mines, foundries and rail yards, getting no compensation (because, it was argued, they worked there by choice). This is what the Populists battled. The battle was rough and long, with repeated strike actions, poverty and despair for workers.

Laissez-faire, the philosophy of robber barons, was eventually collared and muzzled, notably in Supreme Court decisions headed by Justice Brandeis who saw unfettered business practices as an eventual threat to democracy. It took many years to produce a real turn. The Seattle General Strike of 1919 was another attempt to break through.

Eventually both Social Darwinism and *laissez-faire* were abandoned.

Spirited

Laissez-faire is rising again.

The Libertarian Party, formed in 1972, looks New Age-ish. Libertarians promises a bright new beginning, the kind of thing that always attracts young people with spirited talk about freedom from authority. In fact libertarians almost never stop talking about freedom.

Libertarians believe this: individualism is what a society is all about. The promotion of self, and self-interest, life, liberty and property rights are important. Businesses and markets should also be free from restraint. Libertarianism hates constraint. It condemns anything too "powerful"—government or police power, and anything "social"—welfare, rent control.

Here are its founding assumptions. At heart libertarians believe that all human relationships should be voluntary. They think there is a natural harmony of interests among people, and any society works by a sort of spontaneous order.

In politics, libertarianism claims to be against both the left wing and the right. It states opposition to fundamentalist religion as much as against any state agency—both threaten individual freedom.

How do we know the old ideology of *laissez-faire* is in here? Because a 1997 book which explains the basics, by David Boaz (executive vice president of the Cato Institute) called *Libertarianism: A Primer* says so. It states that *laissez-faire* capitalism is the answer to everything because it brings incredible wealth to all. And it proudly champions Adam Smith's ideas as its heritage *(34)*,.

Justice in Two Pages

Those founding assumptions are nonsense. First it's obvious not all people are interested in harmony. Some are excessively greedy. Some people prefer power, which tends to corrupt. Second, world history books show few human societies working smoothly by spontaneous order.

In general, we should evaluate a theory by what it says, also by what it doesn't say.

What does *Libertarianism* say about exploitation? Nothing. The word isn't even in the index.

Next, its treatment of justice is negligible. And what does it say about equality?—Almost nothing. It is hard to convey libertarianism's disinterest in equality. Or perhaps this: Boaz's book has 314 pages. Just over one page is given to equality. Equity?—nothing. Justice?—under two pages.

Consider a modern concern. What about big-business abuse of the environment? Among other points in the book—to give environmentalists nightmares—is that libertarians see no contradiction between industry expansion and the environment. Quote: "Economic growth helps to produce environmental quality." *(35)*

Reading *Libertarianism* reveals something much more troubling. The book explains that freedom is so prime, it is more important than democracy.

Libertarianism is disinterested in democracy. Rather, libertarians believe in Natural Law, laws seated in ancient, even tribal, crude customs, which are hardly enlightened ways. There is actually a fringe element among libertarians, gaining momentum, which seriously wants to dismantle democracy in America *(36)* which it interprets as mob rule.

While this style of business in the 1890s, for profits, freely harnessed uneducated millions of the poor into sweatshops and mills, at wages that always seemed to keep them frightened and hungry, all those problems are now forgotten by libertarians—as if the century had no shadow.

And without a twitch of embarrassment a *Chicago Tribune* review on the dustcover of Boaz's book *Libertarianism* explains that "these are ideas that are coming to dominate the thinking of government all over the world."

Tinsel

Laissez-faire is critical for today's aggressive corporations because they cannot operate at their gargantuan level without almost total freedom. Corporate businessmen cite as their biggest enemy, government. They see greed as a solution rather than a problem. They despise the push for equality as a death-knell. They refer to justice as something the envious dreamed up *(37)*. For them democracy is no more than a bright tinsel wrapping to be torn off the moment it poses any real constraint around their freedom.

Bang

Despite these concerns, our market economy is not weakening in any way.

The reverse. At this point in history capitalism is just getting started on a second Big Bang. We are recently launched into another expand-or-die wave that dates back approximately to the fall of the Berlin Wall and is already showing geometric power. It's being promoted by our massive gifts and loans to foreign countries, by our placing key capitalists in international banking. And, less benevolently, by the starting of foreign wars, which require repairs, for which we provide contractors, whose profits return to us.

This new wave is not powered by any single ideology. But this odd combination of Social Darwinism and *laissez-faire* is a soil mixture that produced the explosive capitalism and empire-building at the turn of the last century, and it will work again.

I say odd combination because these two theories are actually contradictory. Libertarians should look over their shoulders. Biology promotes the opposite point, that we humans don't have much freedom because our behavior is controlled by our genes. Sociobiologists say even the functioning of our societies is constrained by our genes, so the idea of us choosing to expand our liberties is hilarious to them.

These two theories were also contradictory a hundred years ago. That didn't stop monopolists then and it will not stop the high-octane business leaders of today—none of whom are exactly intellectuals.

Exalted

Turn on the television and watch our national leaders talk policy. They explain we are bringing our way of doing business to foreign lands because capitalism brings democracy. We are the bringers of fortune, uplift, goodness, opportunity and freedom for all—the best destiny humanity has to offer.

Just because this argument is delivered from a podium bathed in rotating lights does not make it true. It is also broken logic.

One of the main events in capitalism is the creation of inequality.

We recall that the two basic values of democracy are freedom and equality. They are the two wings on which that exalted bird flies.

And we notice these official speeches on foreign policy promise freedom, but they never promise equality. We cannot export equality. You cannot give away what you haven't got.

Second, a point always omitted from these speeches is that capitalism comes in different species. One type is *authoritarian capitalism* and it is decidedly undemocratic. A governing power, sometimes a military dictator, promises businessmen they will make astonishing profits if they just follow his orders. This—the melding of business and state—happens to be one of the elements of fascism. Another defining element of fascism is that inequality is a virtue.

But free market economies are being built everywhere. This new wave is so powerful, it has the face of a titan.

So we cannot do it any harm, analyzing it. We have plenty of time to pull up our chairs, and at our leisure examine its beating heart.

Corporations

The major musculature of our modern free markets is corporations. They deserve attention.

Corporations are collections of people doing business. Other types of business entities exist, sole proprietorships and partnerships, but corporations are surely the largest. (Some corporations are more wealthy than some countries). They inspire joy in some people, fear in others.

Corporations have been harshly attacked in several books by investigative reporters. For example Mokhiber and Weissman's *Corporate Predators* and Court's *Corporateering* warn of the way corporations influence politics (by shifting massive capital around) as well as the way they take away our personal privacy and security. As a rule they lack transparency. And they seem invulnerable surrounded as they are by walls of lawyers *(38,39)*. Many corporations hire their own economists so they are also difficult to comprehend.

These books are a good and healthy part of the public's reading. But these attacks have made no difference.

One book, however, written by a lawyer, may make a difference. It translates the stygian legalese and economics into common language. The book is no less frightening.

The author reveals the corporate Achilles heel.

Bodies in Two Parts

Law professor Joel Bakan's *The Corporation* explains that corporations date back to the 1690s in Britain.

From the start corporations were peculiarities, being bodies that are split into two parts. Directors and managers run the firms, but stockholders own them. And the stockholders are an ever shifting bunch, being owners today, sellers tomorrow.

Most stockholders have no interest in how the firm does business. They only look at the daily value of the stock. Since the only business of a corporations is to make profit, this is a recipe for corruption because the stock's value can fluctuate on rumor and reputation, and a firm might grow wealthy on lies, or by overcharging, or by selling a dangerous product, or by not doing anything except issuing promises, and the stockholders are just as delighted. Stockholders don't ask questions.

Second, the corporation has "a legal mandate to pursue, relentlessly and without exception its own self interest" and this "regardless of the harmful consequences it might cause others." If along the way they have to pay some fines for damage they have done, this is calculated into business expenses. It's all numbers. And since some corporations make massive profits, they don't flinch at paying out very large sums to people and environments they have damaged very badly. And then return to do it again.

Anything that is an unfortunate byproduct of making profit, such as stress, lives lost, disease, broken laws, pollution, immorality, 'collateral damage,' grief, disruption, riots, is called an 'externality' because it is outside the crisp equation for calculation profit and loss. Most of what we know as morality and humanity are externalities.

This breakage can have enormous effects on the world. Corporations are externalizing machines, says Bakan, bulldozing through to more profits. They routinely break stuff wherever they go and this single-mindedness has produced what we have today, colossuses of indifference "of such power as to weaken government's ability to control them," so that "corporations now govern society perhaps more than governments do."

Yes, there are some corporation CEOs who exercise morality and judgment. But they are not supported by Nobel Prize winning economist Milton Friedman, who believes the only moral duty of the corporation is to put profit over social and environmental goals (and business guru Peter Drucker thinks likewise).

Bakan goes further. He likens corporations to psychopaths (sociopaths). For his book he interviewed Dr. Robert Hare, a psychologist and expert on psychopathy, to get a list of personality traits that psychopaths exhibit (no empathy, asocial behaviors, manipulativeness, no conscience, no remorse) and then tries those out on corporations. They fit. For instance corporations return repeatedly to make profits from things they know are lethal and that strew grief—cigarettes, cars that catch fire in crashes, drugs with devastating side effects—because the money is there. Enough money gives them a "psychopathic contempt for legal constraint." Or any constraint. Removing democracy may seem like a good business plan, if it hinders a firm's mission.

In corporate culture there is an emerging social order that is wide and dangerous, as dangerous as any fundamentalism, Bakan states. "For in a world where anything or anyone can be owned, manipulated, and exploited for profit, everything and everyone will eventually be."

Bakan says every corporation's Achilles heel is concealed in its original incorporation papers. I will return to this point in the later section on remedies *(40)*.

Odd Folks

If corporations are really like that, we might wonder about the people who work in them. Tens of millions of regular folks work in corporations, of course, which gives them the surface look of well fed averageness. But because of their aggressive business agenda, they also attract some odd personalities.

Psychopath

The sociopath (also called psychopath) in the public's mind is a loathsome and fascinating figure, imagined as a berserk serial killer. Actually, most sociopaths couldn't be more different. Suave and charming, manicured starters of conversations, many look like they come from the pages of *GQ*. (There are plenty of lissome women sociopaths too.) Consummate actors, you melt when they talk to you. They are smooth as glass. They exhibit a tapered arrogance. They are also "persistent, repetitive, remorseless violators of the rights of others, and the rules of society" *(41)*.

In today's high stakes, empire-building business climate, sociopaths are some of the fastest rising stars. In corporate maneuvering they have no loyalty, virtually no emotion, and no conscience. Promiscuous in friendships as in sex, they start instantly and leave an alliance instantly it creates advantage. Their specialty is stirring and steering feelings in others without being touched themselves. Usually the epitome of self control, they are capable if cornered of sudden viciousness. Few will challenge them, sensing that underneath is their calculated enjoyment of the destruction and humiliation of others.

This is not a new type of personality. But in modern culture, where success has become separated from honor, they thrive. The sole passion they have is to win. The particular combination of sociopathy and high intelligence is a prototype for business success.

Harvard's psychopathy expert Martha Stout estimates about 1 in 25 people are these indifferent, charismatic liars and the proportion is growing. You may have one at your picnic; there was one in your classroom at school; at one time you probably tried to date one.

Stout sketches a prototype sociopath growing up. He came from a privileged city family and stole from his parents. He enjoyed stuffing live firecrackers down frogs' throats. He was so intelligent he cruised through college almost without studying and, graduating with an MBA, he was quickly hired by a large corporation, where he proved he could sell anything. "Lying comes as easily as breathing," and despite subordinates complaining that he is insulting and vicious he starts on a meteoric ascent, marries a sweet, quiet woman, and before middle age is given a division presidency. He makes many millions of dollars for the company and enjoys his female subordinates as sexual plunder.

Stout explains the brains of sociopaths work differently. Watched through brains scans, normal people, given words to think about, quickly process emotional words like "love" and "happy," but sociopaths are a bit slower because they process emotions in the temporal lobe where most people solve algebra problems.

High Mating Effort

Stout also says there is a genetic base. Sociopathy runs in families and is partly hereditary. She estimates about 50 percent of it is inborn *(42)*.

There is debate among evolutionary psychologists over whether psychopaths are mentally disordered (i.e. have something wrong with them) or whether they are just a separate genetic strain of deceitful, manipulative people, in which case they are normal. If it is a disorder, psychopaths are notoriously difficult to treat (they don't voluntarily come in for psychotherapy, and if required to, they don't change). Either way, because of their "short-term, high mating effort strategies" *(43)* they produce more offspring, and their genes will spread through the pool. From an evolutionary point of view, this type is becoming more common.

Intimidation

Our culture is unwilling to stop them. We furiously promote these smooth surfaced, antisocial people when they turn their talents to making money for the company. Then as CEOs and CFOs we give them extraordinary business power. In that position, the law supports them, because (as above) current law says the corporation has "the legal mandate to pursue, relentlessly and without exception, self interest, regardless of the often harmful consequences" *(44)*.

Wrap this all around in the ruthless ideology of Social Darwinism, and nobody is safe. Democracy itself is not safe.

Democracy is something a sociopath loathes, because it represents public constraint by 'little people' on his autocratic power. And he doesn't practice democracy inside corporate walls. What he often practices in the corridors and boardrooms is coercion and intimidation. Returning to Conniff's observations: "Great fortune builders are also often great screamers [who use] the diatribe as a favorite tool...He calls meetings...at which he rages, growls and curses at his weary employees" *(45)*.

Why is this type so successful? One possibility: because these malignant personalities are at home in the system. And the reason for that is that the system is malignant.

History contain several examples of sociopaths who have flattened democracies.

Red Ink

Here are some other odd personalities who appear in corporations, as described by Jean Hollands, a business consultant who can calculate the dollar loss due to a valuable employee's bad behavior.

Large corporations sometimes hire high-ranking specialists and managers who come with personal problems which wear everyone down. These people are not just occasional curiosities; they can be found in every large organization. Company owners are aware of these scabrous personalities under the roof, but are startled to find out just how much they are draining the company since their styles affect many other people.

Hollands shows the owners the company they could be making hundreds of thousands of dollars more profit if they got rid of these misfits, but they don't partly because of the expense of firing and rehiring.

In her book *Red Ink Behaviors* she gives illustrations. The Intimidator (loud, domineering, abusing, throws tantrums, but somehow thinks he is funny), the Stressor (severe workaholic, spills her chronic frustration over coworkers in sarcasm and unending interruptions), the Micromanager (requires written reports at every turn which he examines line by line, is chronically overwhelmed by all this work), the Witholder (has data necessary for operations which she will not share, chronically late to meetings or absent), the Inconsistent (thin skinned, high drama, unpredictable hysteric, lapses into stream-of-consciousness communications) and the Techno-specialist (brilliant but won't talk to anyone who's not a technician.)

These personalities are not easy to confront. They are extremely judgmental, to the point of mild paranoia, and if confronted they turn rabid or wall themselves up in their offices which is devastating to company morale, creating ripples of anxiety across the cubicles. And because coworkers usually back away from them, the offenders interpret this as a win, and they do it again. Hollands points out that this event, "winning," is highly valued in high-stakes businesses (sales, legal, brokerage) where competitive individualism is prized, so nobody is sure what to do. So the toxic atmosphere spread by these bullies is borne, and everybody dreads going to work *(46)*.

The Street

Adam Smith never talked about these odd personalities. Adams Smith's main point is that humans are naturally self-centered, and if you allow all people to work in their self-interest, the nation will benefit.

But individual self-interest will not explain everything. You cannot build a successful economy with something like self-interest any more than you can toss a bunch of boards in the air and expect them to come down in the shape of a house. Much is missing.

Which means a search. Requiring a long journey through rarified concepts? No, I believe the search will take us places we already know. And I am swayed by Nietzsche and his habit of scorning academics who want to make things complicated. The great problems of this world, he said, are not in misty metaphysics. They are in the street. Particularly they are in places we don't expect.

We don't care to look down. Is it because that direction is filled with nothing interesting?

The media seems to affirm that. Apparently, time spent on the lives of workers would be gilding a vacuum. If we follow the media, we will always to look up.

That is why we are missing answers.

Organic

A tree's height and the depth are connected. Everybody accepts that because the tree is an organic whole. A building is another kind of organic whole, and if the building is built taller, its foundation must go down. But libertarian economists refuse the heights and depths of our own society to be connected—yes, the rich get richer and the poor get poorer, but that is somehow a coincidence because everybody is free.

In the life of a tree, what happens below determines what happens above. And I believe if we want to understand how an economy creates such high levels of wealth, we will need to look at its soil, and below, even if it is not pretty where the roots are coiling and clenching the rubble everywhere.

What do we hear when we hold our ear to the soil?

Work

We can start with the broad question. Why do we work? It is a fair question.

We want to jump in: "To earn a living," "To support the family," "To get ahead."—All partly true, or true for some people.

Actually the broader question stumps professional analysts. The cover story of a 2003 issue of *US News and World Report* titled "Why we work" wanders around for several pages and is simply evasive, but says: "Some do it for love. Others do it for money. But most of us do it because we have no other choice." *(47)*

That doesn't sound like the freedom shouted up by libertarians.

Worksites

The goal of businesses is product and profit. If American all produced something new in their work, we would be a prodigious and much happier society. In fact, worksites are often not what we would expect. The reality is that huge amounts of work effort are spent overcoming inefficiencies. What inefficiencies? Workers often spend hours trying to find, cleaning up, checking, losing, leaving messages, not connecting with, misunderstanding, delivering to the wrong place, catching up, waiting, repairing, clarifying miscommunications, correcting mistakes—myriad forms of blather and delay—and all exhausted at the end of the day.

So answers to the question "why do we work?" like, to make, or to produce, are part of the myth of work, but to get a little closer to reality we need to look at things the texts books don't talk about.

A part of the answer is supplied by what happens at work.

One thing that never fails to happen on the job is hierarchy. Hierarchy is ever present in manufacturing, service, private, government, military, civilian, inside-work, outside-work, unsuccessful, successful, full time, part time, day, night, sea, land, intense and indifferent jobs. It is much more predictable than—much more reliable across worksites of different kinds than—money, motivation, service, satisfaction, effort, efficiency, profit or product, which vary.

What hierarchy ensures is control. (The *US News* article does point out that although more workers are using their homes, it is no escape from hierarchy—and the phone and emails don't stop after 5:00 p.m.)

Wage

So if I go to work for someone, I will enter some sort of hierarchy. And if I go to work for someone, somewhere, I am also selling my personal freedom for a wage.

So most work sites create the opposite of the two basic values of democracy which are freedom and equality.

This is a dark pond into which nobody ever tosses a stone.

Cheery

Should we say, the more people working, the more satisfied the nation? That would be nice. But realistically, the more people work, the more people are enmeshed in a system of control which is nondemocratic. That's not such a cheery thing to say, but we are tired of having the outside world made cheery by the method of painting our windows blue. If we want to see better, we will have to scrape it off.

Quest

And these topics do not make easy conversation with our co-workers. At this point in our search we'll meet with a lot of silences. We verge on taboo.

Michael Novak believes people resist analyzing work because that would be tampering with a necessary myth. We might find contradictions. Any contradiction would threaten society's foundations. The value of hard, competitive work *is* our society, Novak says. It is painstakingly reinforced from birth and "without that myth our society is inconceivable." *(48)*.

The origins? Generation after generation of young persons are taught that work is the route to personal dignity and worth. For each child this is repeated in one form or another through school and a light is turned on. Success and failure is everything, no ambition is too high. These myths take a deep hold, they have the spiritual power of hope and by the time a school graduate enters the workforce he is ready for something momentous to happen.

So each worker starts out on a personal quest. If he talks to others workers about his dreams of growth and expansion, they smile, and later he notices old workers at his job doing much the same work and he starts to think, and to keep his inner visions quiet. Gradually he sinks into routines. He dodges the inanities and politics of the workplace. After many years, that inner light, once supple and strong, is changed. Work doesn't change much. If the child originally dreamed of being in the NBA or being an explorer, working in an office will feel like a cul-de-sac. But he does the work. He becomes a watcher-of-others. Later perhaps he still has hope, but it is in a different form: now he is darkly working on a distant hope of vindication. Even later he changes again. Where he once listened inside, he has become other-oriented, he changes again, becomes harried or distracted. He works because of obligations, or for security, or for the company. If the light goes out, this is the way he will finish his days, in routines, swimming with all the others, in these vast pools of irrelevant direction. *(49)*

He was from the start harnessed to somebody else's dream.

Nonetheless, as this person grows up he will stir the same myth in his own children.

Snappy

This wreckage of myths is where we do not want to look.

Studs Terkel in 1972 put together a thick book of self-reports entitle *Working*. He interviewed workers of all kinds, proofreaders to nurses, to stockbrokers, to hookers, to jockeys, to welders, to executives, to stone cutters, to accountants, to dentists. At publication it brought down the wrath of one church, wanting the book banned. Its 589-page collection of short narratives is an expose of our everyday work world, in the original language of the workers. This is the introductory paragraph:

"This book, being about work, is, by is very nature, about violence—to the spirit as well as to the body. It is about ulcers as well as accidents, about shouting matches as well as fistfights, about nervous breakdowns as well as kicking the dog around. It is, above all (or beneath all), about daily humiliations. To survive the day is triumph enough for the walking wounded among the great many of us." *(50)*.

This doesn't match Adam Smith's snappy view of the workaday world as busy pin factory workers and energetic vendors hauling goods to market, like bees in a hive. So is it lies?

If Terkel was the only writer, we might come away with thinking he's a hothead. But he's not the only one. More recently a woman from the academic elite used a different method.

Climbing Down

In 1999 Barbara Ehrenreich, who holds a Ph.D. in Biology, tried an experiment. She changed her clothes and climbed down the social ladder to be a person living on minimum wage. This level of society is called the working poor. Being trained as a scientist, she took careful notes. She detailed her experiences in the book *Nickel and Dimed*. One after another she took six jobs, for a minimum of a month each, including waitress, hotel maid, house cleaner, nursing home aide, and WalMart salesperson. She drove a car, but made herself live each month only on what she could earn—mostly at $6 and $7 an hour. This meant living in the cheapest lodgings (trailer parks, motels, downtown hotels) and eating on a narrow, bland diet.

The jobs were available. Once on the job she was an exemplary worker. But her first finding was that it is almost impossible to work for those wages and survive. For instance, monthly earnings as a waitress in Florida were $1,039. The cheapest rental she could find was a $500 efficiency, and food, gas, laundry, utilities and phone and toiletries came to $517, leaving her $22 for everything else. She moved to Maine, hired out as a house cleaner, scrubbing young yuppies' houses, making $6.65, and paying $480 rent for a room, and so on.

Her second finding was that the jobs often involved exhausting effort, and overtime, and in some jobs she literally worked by the sweat of her brow so that all she wanted to do at night was watch TV over her dinner and fall asleep.

Specimen

She became socially invisible—interacting with nobody except her immediate supervisors and coworkers; she felt 'disappeared' from society. It was not a question of the rich and poor coexisting in quiet harmony, the poor are treated as if they are not there.

She endured humiliation, abuse and routine violation of privacy, and sometimes had to surrender basic civil rights. As a waitress she was told that her purse could be search at any time by management. There were rules against talking on the job. Constant surveillance, being written up by the shift supervisor, being 'reamed out' by managers were all customary parts of the job, also being subjected to drug tests in (which in some cases includes stripping to underwear and urinating in presence of a specimen collector.) After a while she felt she was not just selling her labor but her life.

Ehrenreich muses that since the people she was around were all hard workers, there seemed no purpose to the authoritarianism of managers except to create a culture of extreme inequality. Demeaning employees sometimes seemed attractive for employers. The repressive management style also produced the feeling of failure and shame, which, she suspects, keeps down wages because eventually workers think so little of their own worth that they accept the low pay.

Ehrenreich is one writer who has paused by this thought. We have a massive cultural contradiction. "We can hardly pride ourselves on being the world's preeminent democracy, after all, if large numbers of citizens spend half their waking hours in what amounts, in plain terms, to a dictatorship." *(51)*

Meritocracy

To our Western minds, some kinds of inequality are less tolerable than others, less 'fair.'

Actually there is no human society with perfect equality. All cultures contain some inequality and the big question is the criterion, because some reasons for inequality are seen as unjust. For instance America thinks monarchy and inherited aristocracy is wrong, but in neighboring Canada it is accepted. In some communities rank is based on brute strength, in others, pureness-of-heart. Nobody likes to be low on any hierarchy.

Societies with inherited rank also find it's inefficient. The British, for instance, used to give all their top government jobs and high offices to relatives of nobles. The problem was a lot of the nobility and their relatives are not very bright. As a society grows more technological it needs more pure intelligence to run it. So a century ago the British started awarding important positions by qualifying exams and educational achievement, open to anybody.

But there's a benefit to hierarchy by birth: being low is not your fault, and it's not a moral problem.

In America the idea that anybody should be able to rise is old, and a person's position has always depended more on ability and accomplishments. This is meritocracy. Meritocracy seems more democratic. It is appealing because it seems to be all about self-steered destiny.

But by the same token, meritocracy introduces blame for low rank. If you haven't accumulated accomplishments during your life, your low rank is a moral problem because you were free and you had the chance.

In America, therefore, the rich are better, the poor should be ashamed.

All this creates a special set of fears called "status anxiety" by de Botton *(52)* and "fear of sinking" by Kilmer *(53)*, an obsessive concern with social status.

Debt

After all that work at minimum wage, Ehrenreich experienced how it was easy to spend your working life sinking deeper into debt.

Economic indebtedness takes away some of your freedom, but many people who are affluent don't understand money traps, so here I'll spend a few words on a topic that is technically on the consumer side.

Perhaps this will all fall into focus leaf by leaf.

Credit Cards

After decades of aggressively distributing credit cards to virtually anyone who can sign, lenders have worked themselves into a paramount position of power. Now the average person is obligated at about $8,500 in debt. Lenders can charge interest up to 30%. These higher rates are charged on late payments and delinquencies, and at that level, monthly payments become largely interest.

Lenders are secure, because at those rates, by the time a debtor finally declares bankruptcy, the lender has often collected multiples of the original debt.

The lenders are making most of their money from poor people—people who don't have to the money to make prompt payments. Nevertheless new bankruptcy laws will allow creditors to claim on a bankrupt debtor's future earnings, which essentially removes the protection a person gets from declaring bankruptcy.

Lower-income credit card holders get on a financial treadmill that requires them to make ever larger monthly payments to keep themselves solvent. People who are ill, poor, old, on fixed income have all been urged to take credit cards. Then they are largely sealed onto a wheel which never pauses.

Usury

Debt payments are the scourge of the poor but this is a spreading problem and includes an increasing numbers of the middle class.

Many countries have usury laws that control predatory interest rates. In Europe these laws date back centuries. In the United States the laws vary from state to state. Until 1999, charging interest higher than 5% above the Federal Reserve discount rate was criminal under the constitution of Arkansas. But some states have no usury laws, which is why powerhouse Citibank relocated its credit card division from New York (interest cap 12%) to South Dakota, and from there works an interstate credit card business charging as high as the market will bear. Today's trend is for states to loosen their usury laws to attract more banks.

Public opinion is gathering against these lenders. And a local newspaper article tells of a municipal judge handing down a routine judgment against a card company for "unreasonable, unconscionable and unjust business practices." *(54)*

Is collecting high interest rates on loans a hard-work method of making a lot of money? Hardly. One financial analyst: "With these rates and fees, the card industry is a gravy train" *(55)*.

Tweakers

What about the people who declare bankruptcy? Aren't they gamblers, system tweakers, profligate spenders? Rarely. People usually go bankrupt because of severe misfortune. Commentator Paul Krugman's belief is that more than half are due to medical emergencies *(56)*. Actually a Harvard-based study by Warren and Tyagi, the ongoing Consumer Bankruptcy Project, shows only 13% of bankruptcies stem from credit card overspending or from covering bad investments, or the like. Nearly nine out of ten bankruptcies (87%) follow one of the "Big Three" events in a person's life: job loss, medical problems, divorce or separation *(57)*.

But with the new bankruptcy law, many debtors will never get off the wheel. Krugman fears America is gradually returning to a "debt peonage" society, after a practice in the post-Civil War South, in which debtors were forced to work for creditors.

Whispering

For the past few years our national leaders have encouraged us to believe our national destruction is imminent at the hands of an evil foreign enemy. Possibly before that, legal loan sharks will eat us out from within.

Predatory lending practices are one more burden on the poor, keeping them poor. It is very hard for the exploited to escape shame and inescapable debt is one reason for the melancholy that haunts the lowest regions of this society.

Credit companies look resplendent in media commercials, situated high in wind-brushed, glass buildings with whispering elevators, manicured executives and elegant beauties for receptionists.

This industry is banditry.

Is Exploitation Wrong?

If you can make wealth through hard work, you can also make it by getting others to do the work for you—even children get this insight.

Getting other people to work for you is using them. Whether using people is immoral is a debatable question.

If somebody is willing to change a flat tire for me, I am using that person. Nobody sees anything wrong. But isn't that exploitation?

Actually, says ethicist R. J. Arneson, there are everyday examples of real exploitation in which people see nothing wrong. Children exploit their parents for trips to the mall and money to spend. Parents exploit their children getting them do household chores. So it seems exploitation is not always bad. Arneson says the word exploitation has two meanings (1) simply to use somebody—no problem, but (2) if you use them and mistreat them in the process, there may be a moral problem *(58)*.

Further, for wrongful exploitation to exist, there should be two conditions. First, the mistreatment (an injustice); second, the person cannot leave. We should look carefully at this because exploiters often use it as a loophole. But together, mistreatment plus no freedom to leave amounts to oppression.

Again, history is replete. No culture has been free of it, and the revolts, revolutions, mutinies and reformations found in the pages of history books are all accounts of oppression and its overthrow.

But whether exploitation is wrong continues to be argued. Sometimes exploited humans do nothing but adjust. What if the oppression is accepted? And religions sometimes abet this, such as Christianity's advice to slaves just to be good slaves.

Aberration

Karl Marx was the first to open exploitation for economic debate *(59)*. After a brief summary of Marx's points I'll touch on some modern theories.

Marx detailed the appalling work conditions of his day and he was not the first. Ferguson *(60)* Ruskin *(61)* and Dickens in his classics also portrayed workers at mind-destroying work in thundering foundries, weather-torn fields, slippery meat houses, 14 hours a day, six days a week, and forced overtime; all for trickle-thin wages, and all accompanied by routine abuse from foul overseers, capricious fines, and often, at these wages only floor space to sleep and bread and soup to eat and ragged clothes—in all a bestial lifestyle, but in all the same, across cities and farms, workers were paid just enough to survive. (Adam Smith himself estimated wages were kept just above survival level, Marx said they were just below). And since the employers also owned the rentals and the stores, the money workers made frequently went back into the same pockets it came from and the laborers found themselves in a trap from which they could never rise.

Here's the way it goes, Marx said. Laborers produce things. Being poor they can only rent out their labor. They have to use their employer's tools or land or raw materials. The product of their toil is taken from them by the employer who then sells it for as much as he can, and turns round and pays the employee as little as he can in wages, because the difference is profit and the mission of capitalists is to maximize profits. Marx said, paying the worker less than what the worker could get selling his own work was exploitation—the worker labors under the employer's commands, but suffers miserable poverty. This, Marx goes on, is not an aberration. It is a routine part of capitalist operations *(62)*.

Marx could discuss everything capitalists talk about, profit margins, the utilitarian greatest good, risk, stockholders, overhead, economies of scale and the expansion of industry. But he picked up the whole situation by a different handle. He said, exploitation is immoral.

Capitalists protested, work is a free exchange. The workers are in our factories by choice—so where's the oppression?

Marx said in practice the workers are not so free to leave because the wealthy owners of factories and farms across the land roughly match each others' wages and rents. So in practice the worker can do no better by moving. In all, labor is sealed into a large closed system. The system is oppressive. It is also to the benefit of the employer class, who do very well.

Energetic

If you are forced to work, that is called coercion. Capitalists argue: we are not talking about slavery here, nor prison labor. Signing on to work with us is a consensual act. Marxists throw back: but these workers are constantly in debt due to your starvation wages, and this amounts to economic coercion because each person is obliged to try to clear his debts. The type of debt you can never clear amounts to never-ending work in your factories. Where's the freedom?

And another thing, Marx went on. Notice how property ownership is connected. The exploiters have the factories and the tools, the exploited don't. Since property ownership is one mark of social class, we have the 'haves' exploiting the 'have-nots.' Marx asserted this: property itself is a moral problem. And since the property-ownership system is wholly supported by the law it's not going to be easy to change.

Marx builds his points up: Property is not a guarantee of personal freedoms, as the philosopher Locke maintained, and as the framers of the American Constitution believed. Property is a legal instrument of oppression. And there is class warfare.

Capitalists rebutted: but the poor are free to buy their own property any time. Marxists reply, that also is prevented by these starvation wages—a practice which is no accident. It is deliberately in the capitalist's interest to keep a large supply of people poor, desperate and willing to work dirt cheap. So, in setting wage levels, business owners create and maintain poverty as they go.

Poverty is also powerlessness. Labor was always negotiating without power, which explained their misery.

Marx was an energetic writer and he used words like "theft" and "embezzlement" to describe employers taking what their employees made. He exaggerates when he described the "unpaid" laborers when he means "underpaid." But Marx also said: all this has got to change. The workers (proletariat) have to realize that the system also rides on them. Without the workers it collapses. So the workers should seize power.

Which led to revolutions. Entire national social structures last century were overturned. Because Marx's points were clear. They show that the less the workers are paid, the greater the success of business owners. They show that a moral wrong, exploitation, can be routinely inserted in economics formulas, and they still work.

Modern Additions

Marx got it the topic started, but other political scientists have added on to it *(63)*.

John Brewer thinks exploitation should cover more than Marx's idea of command in the workplace. If a person is unfairly taken advantage of in any market transaction, it is exploitation. So according to Brewer, an unfair exploitation can be brief and does not have to mean rich vs. poor. Exploitation involves a person receiving lack of just deserts *(64)*.

R.J. van der Veen adds that exploitation is not just a feature of capitalism. It is just as possible for exploitation to occur under socialism and communism if the state commands the individual which work to do, pays him what the state thinks he needs, and if he winds up mistreated and not free to exit *(65)*.

Robert Goodin states that behind the whole notion of exploitation is the expectation in a civilized society that we practice fair play. It's alright to go for advantage against others who are roughly equal. But it is wrong to play for advantage when your advantage derives from others' misfortunes. Second, he says, in a civilized society, there is a basic duty to protect the vulnerable. Exploitation is violating this duty *(66)*.

Ancient

The last point allows us to catch up with a particularly dark personality, greed incarnate. This employer thinks he is his money. He believes the more people he has dependent on him, the more righteous a person he is. So he employs a lot of people and wants to hear all their gratitude. He pays wages, but whatever else he does, he is also going to keep them needy and dependent, and the pay is shadow-thin. This ancient personality may be young, may look excessively healthy, may play with modern gadgetry and makes modern jokes at high tech parties and he moves through our modern society like a quiet abyss.

Varieties of Fear

Most people think there is no fear in the contemporary workplace. Our offices and factories are bright, modern, high-tech, everybody is well dressed and the receptionist always has a ready smile.

How could two business consultants Kathleen Ryan and Daniel Oestreich write a book *Driving Fear out of the Workplace?* (67). Because the authors have interviews and survey data from their work in 22 modern business organizations showing fear is common. True, American employees are not afraid of being slugged, ambushed in the restroom or assaulted in the parking lot unless they work as teachers in inner city schools. But in the nation's factories and office buildings there is fear of other varieties. And most workers are not afraid of the customers or clients. The source of their fear is supervisors and managers.

Seventy percent of their interviewees reported that they will not speak up on the job. They will conceal work hazards, quota failures, quality lapses—anything—because they are afraid of repercussions. What kind of repercussions? Depending on the firm and the manager, anything from refusal to answer and glaring eye-contact ("the look"), to public criticisms, to yelling, insults, threats, tantrums, demotion, being written up as a whiner or troublemaker, to loss of the job. The result is that when managers call workers in to meetings to ask for feedback, or reports, or policy sessions, the workers sit around the table in frigid silence—pure anxiety.

Ulcer

Ryan and Oestreich's analysis shows the more fear there is in a company, the less it is talked about. In Chris Argyris's words, fear seems to be self-sealing. An extreme example would be the military, where hierarchy is absolute, and any lower-rank soldier knows harsh repercussions would fall on him for speaking out—but fear itself is never admitted. Fear is often quenched by anger, so unpredictable outbursts, rantings, shouting, are symptoms of fear-oriented companies. Third, they say, the more fear-based an organization, the more it will make claims to be efficient, systematic and rational—it defines any emotion as irrelevant, so fear is denied or ignored. Still other companies treat fear as an externality. (Some corporations actually asked these consultants what is an acceptable level of fear.)

Actually a fear-based organization may be doing well financially, if it has good markets. But other things being equal, these authors say, fear loses you profits. Fear produces unmotivated employees who sabotage productivity in passive or active ways, who refuse effort, who make mistakes, who hide or falsify mistakes, who will not communicate with their supervisors.

Other symptoms are slow to appear. Some effects of fear are gradually accumulating. Threats and insults may make employees work harder in the short run but in the long run will produce absenteeism, loss of creativity, depression, sleeplessness, crying, tension, ulcers and illness. These are very difficult to reverse. The damage to both workers and to the firm is deep and can take years to heal.

Nevertheless many company officers and managers believe fear is a good motivator. Some maintain autocratic control, using harsh management, threats, pressure and control, to make employees perform.

Self-interest

How does this all start? Ryan and Oestreich's theory says in the beginning management assumes that workers operate from a philosophy of self-interest. The next step is distrust, because management starts thinking the others will try to achieve its self-interest at company's expense. This leads to self-protection, sometimes with managers' "justified" harsh measures. Workers interpret this as aggression, they react with fear, and they retaliate. A cycle is started. It will escalate.

The basic formula is that assumptions of self-interest eventually lead to fear.

Naturally in fear-based groups there is no trust. Instead, owners and managers aggressively demand loyalty.

The therapeutic goal is to reestablish trust in the organization. This is not easy. Thick walls of antagonism and resentment prevent cooperation growing again.

Naive

Ryan and Oestreich's points are clear enough. But they are naïve when they say that management starts out by "adopting" this assumption of self-interest. Actually, management has little choice. Anyone who has survived a course in college Economics 101 or Business 101 is indoctrinated with this assumption of self-interest, because it at the core of our founding economic theory which has hardly been touched since 1776 and which saturates business theory. Any manager who has been to school considers it straight thinking.

Many-footed

Which puts a new contour on things.

If the assumption of self-interest leads to fear, then Adam Smith's theory, which rests on self-interest, is responsible for spreading vast amounts of fear, for eons, for miles, and into the depths of the spirit of the workaday world. And the many-footed formulas of economists do not change that. Anyone who employs other people and uses these assumptions to maximize profits, is a promoter of these vile "externalities." Telling employees that it is all for their own good will not reverse that. The employer protesting that he is uplifting the community, bringing in business, manufacturing and sales, does not reverse it. If we believed those protests, we would have to believe that fear is uplifting for business and uplifting for everybody's life, and so ultimately, being patriotic.

In these worksite accounts democracy looks remote.

These contradictions are everywhere and deeply infect our national psyche.

If you want to remove all the fear, you'll first have to change the overarching Adam Smith theory.

Bragging

I have readers here who do not believe there is fear in the workplace. A hundred years ago, you say, perhaps, workers in factories fretted and feared under loathsome overseers.

The following description is from yesterday's newspaper. It describes work conditions in an existing mortgage loan office in suburban Minneapolis. Sales employees work the phones hour after hour. They sit in rows of cubicles. They are cold-calling, trying to find house-buyers to sign up for sub-par mortgages. The company owner is a billionaire. The company's stated mission includes helping their customers enhance their quality of life. And what is it like working inside the walls of the company's offices?—By the testimony of one ex-employee, it is endless goading by bosses, "Sales agents would work the phones hour after hour...trying to turn phone calls into mortgages. The demands were relentless: one manger prowled the aisles between decks like 'a little Hitler,' hounding agents to make more calls and push more loans, bragging that he hired and fired people so fast that one worker would be cleaning out his desk as his replacement came through the door." Another employee from the same office: "[It's managers] really are all about making the dollar and dealing with the consequences later." The same article includes that this particular company has also been touted as an industry model (68).

Abuse

These managers aren't waiting for the theories of Darwin to explain that injustice is in the nature of things. They are taking things into their own hands.

Of course, the workers are always free to leave.

But if we don't have the money to pay our debts? We are legally obliged to pay our debts. So that freedom fades.

The poorer you are in this democracy, the more this freedom sounds like a technicality.

Or perhaps we self-delude. Our desire for freedom sometimes leads us to see things the way we want, somewhat along these lines by poet Fernando Pessoa: "Inside the coop where he'll stay until he's killed, the rooster sings anthems to liberty because he was given two roosts" *(69.)*

If Adam Smith was right, then all the people in this nation who don't like their work are maximizing their happiness by choosing between the dread of no income or the dread of endlessly going in to work they despise. This is a slender improvement in happiness. Both choices inhabit the region of fear. It is a strange political economy we have that stands on this slender ledge and yells, freedom.

Millions of the undereducated, poor, or vulnerable do unending menial jobs, and are told they can follow their life dreams, and told they can rise, when they never have the power. Millions of Americans struggle and suffer trying to make ends meet and find themselves diverted for life, paying debts.

And will abused workers leave?

Heresy

This psychological research is haunting.

Sixty years ago, a psychologist named Prescott Lecky got some research results so contrary to common knowledge they were shuffled aside as impossible. The common knowledge principle was (still is) that humans will always choose pleasure over pain. Lecky found people suffering with low self-concepts are the exception, they seek confirmation of their low belief in themselves—which is to say, given a choice, they will rather be in the company of a person who puts them down.

In 1945 this little bit of heresy expired quickly and psychology pushed ahead believing people with low self-concepts should all the more hungrily seek reward and pleasure. Lecky's findings were junked.

But fifteen years ago William Swann and his colleagues decided to give the idea another shot. After several new, independent experiments were run it turns out Lecky was right.

A typical experiment goes like this (they vary in detail). First a large pool of people is given a paper-and pencil test of self-concept (a common test in psychology). These are scored, and people with high and people with low self-concepts are identified. Later on these individuals are contacted asked to come in and participate in an apparently unrelated study. When each one comes in, he is asked to sit down and write a personal essay about himself, about a page. Next, a person they've never seen before comes in the room. He comes over, picks up the essay. He reads it, and either exclaims (depending on the flip of a coin just before he came in the door), Well I can see from your essay you've got a great personality, honest, intelligent, popular—or—Well I can see from your essay you're not so great, not very bright, unpopular, also a phony. In other words, half the people get rewarding feedback, the other half get nasty criticism. Now comes the main point in the experiment. All of the essay writers are asked how much more time they would like to spend with the person who read their essay. Results? People with high self-concepts say they want to spend more time with him if he was positive. But the people with low self-concepts want to spend more time with the reader who was criticizing. It appears they choose more pain over pleasure. Apparently, more important than pleasure is to be with somebody who verifies the way you see yourself. "Yeah, that's pretty close to the way I am," and "He sums up pretty close to the way I feel," were typical explanation for the choices of people who felt low about themselves. This effect is especially marked in depressed people *(70,71,72)*.

Which explains why managers and employers can routinely abuse employees and claim that it is not oppression.

If workplace supervisors abuse, then take advantage of this quirk in human nature when the employees return for the next shift, to claim there is no wrong, then no matter how profitable, it is a perversion.

Conspiracy

I have not mentioned the topic of race. Race has been, and still is, a chronic source of debilitating problems.. But we are conditioned to think about social problems in terms of race, so for instance, when we read "underclass" we reflexively think, inner city blacks. Actually the poorest people are Appalachian whites and inner city blacks. They are the lowest class, but Americans have been discouraged from using class to understand anything (Noam Chomsky says if you talk about social class they label you a conspiracy theorist *(73)*).

So to take up Wellesley College's Marcelus Andrews's new argument, which focuses on race and capitalism, seems inconsistent in this essay, and I find Andrews's *Political Economy of Hope and Fear* difficult in parts. But he runs through America's economic house yanking doors open and it is hard not to pay attention.

Goad

Andrews: For hundreds of years we have assumed race and poverty go together (poor equates with 'other races') so we may be surprised to learn that today, the largest group of very poor people in America are whites, and their numbers are increasing. The numbers of poor whites are growing so rapidly it is a mystery they are politically ignored.

Poor people of all races now have little chance of ever making it up to the middle class—for a complex of reasons including economic: the loss of jobs as capitalism goes global; technological: the sudden demands of computer skills at work; and attitude: Americans are really unsure if they want to provide equality of opportunity, because they believe a market economy thrives better on inequality.

Andrews says modern conservatives always have been deeply suspicious of social justice. They are now openly opposed to welfare. They are going to let poverty be a goad.

Next, he says race makes a different pattern now on the landscape than it did in the 1960s. Blacks have more than proved themselves capable, as many, released from the old Jim Crow laws, have climbed and 75% of black families are not poor any more, but the lagging 25% are in a predicament shared by very poor whites. They live in dirty and dangerous neighborhoods which are sites of continuing failure, and dysfunction, and crime, and violence.

Middle-class Americans, who believe in meritocracy, and who cling to myths of self-reliance and freedom, find it difficult to accept the idea of these "poverty traps"—middle class people are always pointing to an ancestor of theirs a century ago who worked their way up from the slums to success—but those were times when education was not a requisite. With today's technology a poor education really is a suffocating disability. And that is what the poor get in these neighborhoods. But that is interpreted as the free market.

With selling drugs and selling sex always an alternative, the poor inhabit the underside of the same free market where there is misery and death. The rest of America, believing its system of meritocracy should be universally applied, accepts that fate as the penalty for lack of ability, education and willingness to work.

Camps

Andrews continues. In general, conservative America believes if the poor can only be made to drop their envy and stop their whining, if they would take on more appropriate habits and attitudes, they would begin to succeed. They believe the poor are behaving badly.

Hearing that feelings of despair and inferiority are unequally distributed does not move conservatives. Under meritocracy, it is just deserts. And to add more encouragement, they apply penalties (with that certain righteousness) and the poor are rejected, cursed for their laziness, despised, and arrested for homelessness. That creates fear, because in fact they cannot leave—first because the poor are discriminated against, just as blacks are—and second they are not *all* free to leave their failure behind because of the nature of meritocracy. Meritocracy is a system in which some must fail.

Resentment and hostility boil in the underclass, which the rest of society dreads and it sends in police with nightsticks ("punishment is by its very nature the deliberate use of public power to inflict pain on offenders") and the feelings and the alienation only grow worse.

Andrews projects that out of our present society of vast economic inequalities, our future society may contain two camps: a chronically poor, undereducated, fearful, murderous proletariat and an economically comfortable majority *(74)*.

Sum

I could use the milder word and say anxiety is a persistent part of the lower reaches of the economy. It is better to be honest and call it by its real name.

I am not arguing the poor are colonized by wealthy employers and lenders in the market system of work-and-debt, but if I wanted to make that argument, there is plenty of ammunition. Our economy runs on a good deal of fear, including fear-of-consequences, which is missing from current economic theory. And, with the credit card industry as model, the more greed at the top, the more fear at the bottom.

Some people turn their eyes. Others actually prefer it that way.

It is in the interest of our economy, at least of the top rungs of business, to maintain this anxiety.

With most people working and with most work places being undemocratic, we may wonder about our aggregate claim to democracy. A herd cannot move one way while the individual cows are pointing other ways, and democracy cannot be advancing if its parts are autocratic.

We don't have equality. Preserving what freedom and what justice we have will take eternal vigilance.

Fear does to a nation what it does to a business. It may be a short term motivator. In the long run fear is debilitating. It is an enzyme of decomposition and dissolution.

Even when Darwinists say fear and hierarchy are unavoidable parts of a dog-eat-dog world, we can press for justice. We always have. We have been fighting injustice, and winning sometimes, as long as we've existed and we should not let the authority of science shut us up.

We want our morality back.

Remedies

I'll make two suggestions. The first is quite whimsical.

White feather. The origins of this idea are in history. During the First World War in England military conscription was used to fill out the Army, but some members of the home community also tried to make sure all young men volunteered. Young ladies walked around public places giving out a white feather to any man in civilian dress. The feather symbolized cowardice and betrayal the country. This was effective. It was considered so shameful to be handed a white feather in public that very, very few men refused military service.

I do not support conscription. But the point is that both greed and cowardice are both considered moral vices, and the idea is to give a white feather to instances of conspicuous greed.

Three strikes. The folks in the State of California have enthusiastically voted to keep a penalty system which puts a person convicted of crime three times in prison for life, the idea is to keep repeating law breakers out of circulation. Recalling the book on corporations by law professor Bakan, he states the Achilles heel of these massive companies is in their articles of incorporation. Under the law, a company's articles can be revoked and it has to cease doing business. Should 'three strikes' be applied to corporations as well? Some corporations do damage. Some are persistent violators of the public trust. Perhaps three convictions (or three public interest law suits lost) should be the limit, and their corporate articles revoked.(For information internet articles on this issue can be retrieved at footnotes 75 and 76.)

THE NUTS GAME: A CONCISE COMMONS DILEMMA ANALOG [1]

Concern over depletion of the world's vital resources has provoked a limited number of experimental investigations by social and environmental psychologists to determine what psychological factors are involved in the mismanagement of resource pools (see Edney & Harper, 1978) for a review). Although laboratory work on this topic is recent, indications are strong that the processes of the tragedy of the commons (Hardin, 1968) can be captured in experimental form using small groups and contrived tasks. Computerized analogs (e.g., Brechner, 1978; Cass & Edney, 1978) have been developed as well as non-computer methods (e.g., Edney & Harper, 1978a, 1978b) but the latter require nonportable apparatus. Other, simpler apparatus have also been reported (e.g., Watzke et al., 1972), some of which are time-consuming to run. This note describes an apparatus for a game which embodies the dynamics of the commons problem. It is simple, portable, easy to operate, and allows manipulation of a number of independent variables as well as the collection of a number of dependent variables. Experimental trials are also short.

Essentially a commons problem occurs when a community of consumers consumes resources at a rate high enough to endanger the regenerating resource itself. Most resources that are living, and many that are not, are liable to overexploitation, and the consumers face the choice of restricting their own consumption for the good of the pool and the community, or continuing to consume at self-satisfying rates to face dire consequences at a later time.

This problem can be operationalized in the following form, paralleling the commons dilemma in many ways. A small number of subjects (three or more) sit around a shallow, nonbreakable, open bowl (convenient diameter 12 inches) which initially contains 10 hardware hexagonal nuts (half-inch diameter is convenient). An experimenter sits with the group and introduces the exercise as one where the player's goal is to get as many of the nuts as possible. Players can take nuts from the bowl at any time and in any quantities after the start of the trial. The experimenter also explains that the number of nuts remaining in the bowl after each 10-second interval is automatically doubled from an outside source (operated by the experimenter, who manually replenishes the nuts from a separate container next to him). This replenishment cycle continues until either an arbitrary time limit is reached or the bowl is emptied by the players. The experimenter can also set a ceiling to the number of nuts in the bowl throughout the trial (10 is convenient). Subjects can be asked not to communicate.

To maximize their individual "harvests" of nuts, one would expect that each subject would restrain himself to taking one or two nuts out of the bowl each 10-second period: this allows the replenishment cycles to continue for some time (a typical game runs 2 minutes) and each subject eventually would end up with a sizeable score. In pilot work I have found that approximately 65% of groups never in practice reach the first replenishment stage because they exhaust the pool by taking all the nuts out in the first few moments of the game.

In this apparatus the bowl symbolizes a resource pool (such as an ocean of whales); the nuts, the resources themselves (these are given real value to the subjects by making them redeemable for money or credit); and the replenishment cycles, natural resource regeneration rates. Taking the nuts is obviously harvesting behavior. As in real-world situations, subjects frequently make the mistake of exhausting the pool by overharvesting, resulting in unnecessarily low scores on each trial. Whatever factors enable subjects to develop a slower harvesting rate (e.g., communication) benefits them all in the long run, and these factors are the focus of experiments as analog methods of determining what prevents resource crises and they form independent variables. Parametric variations of pool size, replenishment rates, value of the nuts, etc., should be easy to explore.

Dependent measures can include (a) individual and group scores (harvest size), (b) number of replenishments or duration of the trial, (c) variance in individuals' harvest sizes, (d) questionnaire items asking subjects for their reactions to the experience, etc., all subject to conventional statistical analysis over a number of trials and/or groups.

Recent pilot work has also shown that the game is unusually involving for subjects. As in the Prisoners Dilemma game (mathematically related to Commons Dilemma games) a fundamental aspect of a good outcome is cooperation among players. Cooperation requires some form of trust in the exercise of mutual restraint, and the evolution and breaking of trusts over the task appears to be an important part of the social dynamics of the exercise.

In pilot testing I have explored a method of running the game in which groups first play the basic game (a majority end up with low scores), then each group is allowed a 5-minute period of free discussion to invent their own rules in order to increase their harvests on a second game, played after the discussion period. The focus here has been on the kinds of rules (methods of play) groups spontaneously generate: these are essentially group-generated attempts at solutions to the commons dilemma. So far, results have suggested two main types of solution: (a) those involving numbers (such as the group which decides systematically to take only "one" or "two" nuts per person per 10-second interval; this type of solution is quite effective in preserving the pool) and (b) nonnumerical solutions. An interesting illustration of the latter was a group which decided deliberately to use a rather complicated system of harvesting. Each player had to hook each nut out of the bowl with a pencil, place it on his nose, walk over to a nearby chalkboard, and deposit the nut in the tray before returning for another nut. Harvesting was thus slowed down enough to prevent pool depletion, increasing individual scores, and incidentally making the game more entertaining to players. The evolution of both kinds of solutions can be regarded as analogs to community-generated laws and practices for direct and indirect governance and management of resources in real-world situations.

In sum the Nuts Game is a practical, manageable, concise, and conceptually defensible form of analog for the study of behavior in resource shortages, and it should lend itself to research in a variety of settings. It might also be conceived of as a teaching device for teaching individuals (such as school children) the value of cooperation in resource management situations. The game's inherent flexibility allows wide variation of parameters and independent variables and makes practical a variety of dependent measures to suit the researcher.

(1) The Nuts Game was originally published by the author in *Environmental Psychology and Nonverbal Behavior*, 1979, Volume 3, pp.252-254. Also described by the author in *Psychology Today*, August 1979, p.80

NOTES: GREED

1. GREED copyright © Julian Edney 2002 and first published on the internet 2003 at www.g-r-e-e-d.com. GREED II copyright © Julian Edney 2005 and first published on the internet 2005 at www.g-r-e-e-d.com.

2. "Fine wines are hot lots at auctions in New York." 2002, *New York Times*, May 27, p. A 12.

3. *Forbes.com Magazine*, 12 April 2001.

4. Reich, Robert B, 1991. "Secession of the successful." *New York Times Magazine*, January 20, p. 16.

5. Galvin, J. "Wretched excess." 2000, *Ziff Davis Smart Business for the New Economy*, August 1, p. 122.

6. "Many miss out on food stamps." 2001, *Los Angeles Times*, June 23. Section B p.1.

7. "3 in 10 Americans face poverty, study says." 1998, *Los Angeles Times*, August 10, Section A p. 15

8. "State picks up house seat as Sunbelt grows." 2000, *Los Angeles Times*, December 29, Section A p.1.

9. Converting old wealth into modern terms is tricky but it appears in 1774 the top 1% owned 14.6% of the national wealth. By 1989 it owned 36.3%. In Gordon J.S. "Numbers game," 1992, *Forbes*, October 9 p 48.

10. Murphey, C. "Are the rich cleaning up?" 2000, *Fortune*, 24 September. p. 252

11. See for example: Childs, J.M. 2000. *Greed*. Minneapolis, Fortress Press, p.36

12. *Los Angeles Times*, 2000, December 12. Section A. p. 1.

13. *Profile of the nation: An American portrait*. 2000, Farmington Hills, MI., Gale Group. P. 180.

14. "Families total 43% of homeless, survey reports." 1993, *Los Angeles Times*, December 22. Section A p. 1

15. Rawls, J. *A theory of justice*. 1971. Cambridge, MA. Harvard University Press.

16. "Study finds widening gap between rich, poor." 2000, *Los Angeles Times* October 20. Section B p.3.

17. Cook, P.J. and Frank, R.H. *The winner-takes-all society: Why the few at the top get so much more than the rest of us*. 1995. New York. Viking Books.

18. Vleminckx, K. and Smeeding, T.M. (Eds) *Child well-being, child poverty and child policy in modern nations*. 2001. Bristol, U.K.: The Policy Press. (Available from the University of Toronto Press.)

19. Durant, W. and Durant, A. *The lessons of history* 1968, New York: MJF Books.

20. Surgeon General aims campaign at rising suicide rate. 2001, *Los Angeles Times* May 3. Section A p. 14.

21. Lasn, K. and Grierson, B. "America the blue." 2000, *Utne Reader*. September. P.74

22. Lane, R.E. *The loss of happiness in market democracies*. 2000. New Haven: Yale University Press.

23. *America Online News*, 2001, by Scott Lindlaw. 10 May.

24. Derber, C. *The wilding of America*. 2002. New York. Worth Publishers.

25. Dostoevsky, F.M. *Notes from underground*. 1864/1992. New York: Bantam Books.

26. "US crime study sees society in trouble." 1999. *Los Angeles Times*. 6 December. Section A p.22

27. Murphy, C. "Are the rich cleaning up?" 2000, *Fortune* 24 September. P. 252.

28. "Is America the land of the poor?" *Investor's Business Daily* 1999, 27 December P. A.1.

29. Freeman, R.B. "Toward an apartheid economy?" *Harvard Business Review* 1996. Sept-Oct p. 114-121

30. Derber, C. Ibid.

31. Childs, J. *Greed.* 2000. Minneapolis, Fortress Press. P. 24.

32. Rawls, J. Ibid, p.33.

33. Bly, R. *The sibling society.* New York: Vintage Books. 1977.

34. Kuhn, H. and Nasar, S. (Eds) *The essential John Nash.* Princeton, N.J. Princeton University Press. 2002.

35. Lasch, C. *The revolt of the elites and the betrayal of democracy.* 1995. New York: Norton.

36. Rose, S.J. *Social stratification in the United States.* 2000, New York: The New Press.

37. McGuire, C. Social stratification and mobility patterns. *American Sociological Review.* 1950, v. 15, p.200. A historical study cited by Gabler found that in 1850, 2 per cent of the wealthy of that period had been born poor while 90 percent were descended from families of affluence and social position: Neal Gabler, *Life: The movie.* 1998. New York: Vintage Books. p. 30.

38. Attributed to Robert Monks, quoted in H. Scutt, *The trouble with capitalism.* New York: Zed Books 1998. P. 176

39. Ryan, R.M. and Deci, E.L. On happiness and human potentials: A review of research on hedonic and eudiamonic well-being. *Annual Review of Psychology.* 2001, 52, 141-166

40. Mark Twain is listed as a caricaturist and a satirist but this does not change my point because the very young do not know enough to distinguish satire (some adults can't either).

41. Sagoff, M. "Do we consume too much?" *Atlantic Monthly*, June 1997, p. 80.

42. Lomborg, B. *The skeptical environmentalist*. 2001. New York: Cambridge University Press.

43. Benedict, R. *Patterns of culture*. 1934/1989 Boston: Houghton Mifflin. The concept of synergy appeared in unpublished lectures Benedict gave in 1941 and all references are derivative, such as M.M. Caffrey: *Ruth Benedict*, 1989 University of Texas Press. p. 308-309

44. Fisher, C.S., Hout, M., Jankowski, M.S., Lucas, S.R., Swidler, A., Voss, K. *Inequality by design*. 1996, Princeton N.J. Princeton University Press.

45. Calabresi, G. and Bobbitt, P. *Tragic choices*. 1978. New York: Norton & Co.

46. Ibid, p. 134

47. Ibid. p. 132

48. Derber, C. *Corporation nation*. 2000. New York: St Martin's Griffin.

49. Lasn, K. and Grierson, B. American the blue. *Utne Reader*, September 2000. p.74.

50. Gabler, N. *Life: the movie*. 1998. New York :Vintage Books.

51. McChesney, R.W. *Corporate media and the threat to democracy*. The Open Media Pamphlet Series. 1997. New York, Seven Stories Press.

52. Ibid.. p. 23

53. "Torture is accelerating globally, report says." *Los Angeles Times*. October 18, 2000. Part A. p. 10.

54. Leonard, G. *Mastery*. 1991. New York: Penguin Books.

55. Adler, A. *The neurotic constitution*. 1926/1998. North Stratford, N.H., Ayer Company Publishers, Inc.

56. See footnote 18.

57. "Foodstamp program is failing in California." *Los Angeles Times* 28 April 2001. p. A 15. A second report is "Many miss out on food stamps" *Los Angeles Times* 23 June 2001. p. B 1. The second article quotes the average food stamp allocation at $73 per person per month.

58. "States cut back coverage for poor." *Los Angeles Times*. 25 February 2002. p. A 1.

59. Food aid programs are administered by the Department of Agriculture. In 2000 total Federal receipts were $1,956,252 million of which $274,448 million went to all food programs, of which the Food Stamp program is one, for which the outlay was $3,392 million. *Statistical Abstracts of the United States.* U.S. Census Bureau, 2000.

60. U.S. Food Assistance (domestic) *The World Almanac and Book of Facts*, 2000. Mahwah, N.J. Primedia Reference, Inc. 2000.

61. *The World Almanac and Book of Facts*, 2000. 2000. Mahwah, N.J. Primedia Reference, Inc.

62. Quoted in "Study finds widening gap between rich, poor" *Los Angeles Times* October 20, 2000. Part B p.3

63. Rawls, J. *A theory of justice.* 1999. Cambridge, MA: Harvard University Press. Revised edition. (The first edition is better, in my opinion.)

64. "The poorest are again losing ground." *Business Week* 23 April 2001, p. 130.

65. "If I'm OK and you're OK, are there any bad guys?" *Los Angeles Times*, 27 January 2002 p. E 1.

66. *Diagnostic and Statistical Manual of Mental Disorders (4th. Ed.)* Washington D.C.: American Psychiatric Association, 1994.

67. J.W. Kalat, *Introduction to psychology.* 6th Ed. Pacific Grove, CA: Wadsworth. 2002.

68. Bruinsma, M. "Culture agents: For closet rebels in the inside game, it's time to speak out." *Adbusters,* Sept/Oct 2001. (Adbusters is unpaged).

69. More recent experimental work focuses on the effects of personal reputation among players: (1) C. Wedekind and M. Milinki, "Cooperation through image scoring in humans," *Science*, 2000, 288, 850-852, and (2) M.A. Nowak, K.M. Page, K. Sigmund, "Fairness versus reason in the Ultimate Game," *Science*, 2000, 289, 1173-1175.

NOTES: GREED II

1. GREED copyright © Julian Edney 2002 and first published on the internet 2003 at www.g-r-e-e-d.com. GREED II copyright © Julian Edney 2005 and first published on the internet 2005 at www.g-r-e-e-d.com.

2. Least affordable rents in nation found in State. *Los Angeles Times*, 21 December 2004. p. C2.

3. Leovy J. A week of painful losses tests police chief's mettle. *Los Angeles Times* 12 Feb 2005 p. A 1.

4. Leonard J, and R Winton, L.A. Jail called deadly, outdated. *Los Angeles Times* 3 Feb 2005. p. A1.

5. Rose, S.J. *Social stratification in the United States*. New York: The New Press, 1992.

6. Those four counties are Wayne, Crawford and Lawrence Counties in Illinois, and Washington County, Florida. In Piutcoff, W., Pelletiere, C., Trekson, M, Dolbeare, C., Crowley, S. *Out of Reach 2004*. Washington DC: National Low Income Housing Coalition, 2004.

7. de Botton, A. *Status anxiety*. New York: Pantheon Books, 2004.

8. Gosselin, P. Credit card firms won as users lost. *Los Angeles Times*, 4 March 2005. p. A1

9. *New York Times 2004 Almanac* (Ed. J. W. Wright). New York: Penguin Reference 2004.

10. Francis, D.R. It's better to be poor in Norway than in the US. *Christian Science Monitor* 14 April 2005. Can be retrieved at: http://www.csmonitor.com/2005/0414/p17s02-cogn.html

11. *New York Times 2004 Almanac* (Ed. J. W. Wright). New York: Penguin Reference 2004.

12. Goodwyn, L. *The populist moment.* New York: Oxford University Press, 1978.

13. *Ibid.* p. 40

14. Lasch, C. *The revolt of the elites and the betrayal of democracy.* New York: Norton, 1996.

15. Derber, C. *The wilding of America.* New York: Worth Publishers, 2002.

16. de Botton, A. *Status anxiety.* New York: Pantheon Books, 2004.

17. Bell, D. *The end of ideology.* Cambridge, Mass: Harvard University Press, 1965.

18. Conniff, R. *The natural history of the rich.* New York: Norton, 2002.

19. Veblen, T. *The theory of the leisure class.* (1899) New York: Penguin Books, 1979.

20. British evolutionist Geoffrey Miller takes this new step in his article "Waste is good." Miller says we have evolved ways of signaling to each other who is more genetically fit—it's who can afford to waste in spectacular ways. A person who uses a pair of £9,652 Sennheiser earphones to listen to music gets almost no better audio quality than someone who uses £25 Vivanco SR250s. The point is, the buyer sees the price as a benefit, not a cost because it publicly shows him different from average people. In other words, Thorstein Veblen's "conspicuous consumption" now gets the nod from Darwinists. G. Miller, "Waste is good." *Prospect.* February 1999. p 18-23.

21. Conniff, p.80.

22. Conniff. p. 24.

23. Salmon, C. The pornography debate: What sex differences in erotica can tell about human sexuality. In C. Crawford and C. Salmon, (Eds.) *Evolutionary Psychology, Public Policy and Personal Decisions.* Mahwah, N.J.: Lawrence Erlbaum Associate. 2004.

24. Shackelford, T.K. and Weeks-Shackelford, V A. Why don't men pay child support? Insights from evolutionary psychology. In C. Crawford and C. Salmon, (Eds.) *Evolutionary Psychology, Public Policy and Personal Decisions.* Mahwah, N.J.: Lawrence Erlbaum Associate. 2004.

25. Thornhill, R and Palmer, C.T. Evolutionary life history perspective on rape. In C. Crawford and C. Salmon, (Eds.) *Evolutionary Psychology, Public Policy and Personal Decisions.* Mahwah, N.J.: Lawrence Erlbaum Associate. 2004

26. C. Crawford and C. Salmon, (Eds.) *Evolutionary Psychology, Public Policy and Personal Decisions.* Mahwah, N.J.: Lawrence Erlbaum Associate. 2004.

27. Dawkins, R. *The selfish gene.* Oxford: Oxford University Press, 1976.

28. Miller, G. "Waste is good." *Prospect.* February 1999. p 18-23.

29. Batson, C.D. Seeing the light: what does biology tell us about human social behavior? *Behavioral and Brain Sciences.* 1994, *17*, 610-611.

30. See this debate in D.S. Wilson and E. Sober. Reintroducing group selection to the human behavioral sciences, *Behavioral and Brain Sciences.* 1994, *17*, 585-654.

31. Nesse, R. M. Why is group selection such a problem? *Behavioral and Brain Sciences.* 1994, *17*, 633.

32. Kennedy, J.G. *Herbert Spencer.* Boston, MA: Twayne Publishers. 1978.

33. Perry, R.J. Sociobiology: science in the service of ideology. *Ethics,* 1980, *91,*125-137.

34. Boaz, D. *Libertarianism: a primer.* New York: The Free Press. 1997.

35. *Ibid.* p. 248.

36. Hoppe, H. H. *Democracy: the god that failed.* New Brunswick, NJ: Transaction Publishers, 2004.

37. This is a favorite theme of Hayek's. F.A. Hayek, *The constitution of liberty.* Chicago: University of Chicago Press, 1960. See p. 93.

38. Mokhiber, R. and Weissman, R. *Corporate predators.* Monroe, ME: Common Courage Press. 1999.

39. Court, J. *Corporateering: How corporate power steals your personal freedom.* New York: Jeremy Tarcher/Putnam. 2003,

40. Bakan, J. *The corporation: the pathological pursuit of profit and power.* Toronto: Penguin Canada, 2004.

41. Barr, K.N. and Quinsey, V.L. Is psychopathy pathology or a life strategy?: Implications for social policy. In C. Crawford and C. Salmon, (Eds.) *Evolutionary Psychology, Public Policy and Personal Decisions.* Mahwah, N.J.: Lawrence Erlbaum Associate. 2004.

42. Stout, M. "The ice people." *Psychology Today.* February 2005. Pp. 72-78.

43. Barr, K.N. and Quinsey, V.L. p.301.

44. Bakan, p.1.

45. Conniff, p. 85.

46. Hollands, J.A. *Red ink behaviors: Measuring the surprisingly high cost of problem behaviors in valuable employees.* Mountain View, CA: Blake/Madsen Publishers, 1997.

47. Curry, A. Why we work. *U.S. News and World Report.* 2003, *34,* 49-52.

48. Novak, M. *The experience of nothingness.* New York: Harper and Row, 1970. p 20.

49. Ibid. p. 21

50. Terkel, S. *Working.* New York: The New Press, 1972.

51. Ehrenreich, B. *Nickel and dimed: On (not) getting by in America.* New York: Henry Holt and Company, 2001.

52. de Botton, A. *Status anxiety.* New York: Pantheon Books, 2004.

53. Kilmer, P.D. *The fear of sinking.* Knoxville: University of Tennessee Press, 1996.

54. Gosselin, P. "Credit card firms won as users lost." *Los Angeles Times.* 4 March 2005. p. A1-24, quote p. 24.

55. Ibid. p A 24.

56. Krugman, P. "The debt-peonage society." *New York Times* Op-Ed. Late edition. Section A. p. 23.

57. Warren, E. and Tyagi, A. W. *The two-income trap.* NY: Basic Book, 2003.

58. Areneson, R.J. "What's wrong with exploitation?" *Ethics,* 1981, 91, 202-227.

59. Marx, K. *Capital. Vol. 1.* (1867). New York: Penguin Books, 1976.

60. Ferguson, A. *An essay on the history of civil society.* (Ed: Oz-Salsberger, F.) Cambridge: Cambridge University Press, 1995.

61. Ruskin, J. *Unto this last.* (1862). New York: Penguin Books, 1985.

62. See also Brewer, J.D. "The Scottish Enlightenment" in *Modern theories of exploitation.* A. Reeve (Ed.). Beverly Hills, CA: Sage Publications, 1987.

63. Reeve, A. (Ed.). *Modern theories of exploitation.* Beverly Hills, CA: Sage Publications, 1987.

64. See 62.

65. van der Veen, R.J. "Can socialism be non-exploitative?" in A. Reeve (Ed.). *Modern theories of exploitation.* Beverly Hills, CA: Sage Publications, 1987. p. 80

66. Goodin, R.E. "Exploiting a situation and exploiting a person." in A. Reeve (Ed.). *Modern theories of exploitation.* Beverly Hills, CA: Sage Publications, 1987. (p. 166)

67. Ryan, K and Oestreich, D. *Driving fear out of the workplace.* San Francisco: Jossey-Bass Publishers, 1998.

68. Hudson, M. and Reckard, E. "Workers say lender ran 'boiler rooms'." *Los Angeles Times.* 4 February 2005. p. A1.

69. Pessoa, F. *The book of disquiet.* London: Penguin Books, 2002. p. 125.

70. Swann, W. B., Stein-Serrousi, A., Giesler, R. B. Why people self-verfiy. *Journal of Personality and Social Psychology.* 1992, *62,* 392-401.

71. Swann, W. B. The trouble with change. *Psychological Science.* 1997, *8,* 177-183.

72. Swann, W. B., Wenzlaff, R. M., Krull, D.S. and Pelham, B. W. Allure of negative feedback: Self-verification strivings among depressed persons. *Journal of Abnormal Psychology.* 1992, *101,* 293-306.

73. Chomsky, N., with Mitchell, P. R. and Schoeffel, J. (Eds.) *Understanding power.* NY: The New Press, 2002.

74. Andrews, M. *The political economy of hope and fear.* NY: New York University Press, 1999.

75. http://www.commondreams.org/views03/0307-02.htm

76. http://www.consumerwatchdog.org/corporate/pr/pr003420.php3

NOTES: THE NUTS GAME

Brechner. K. C. An experimental analysis of social traps. *Journal of Experimental Social Psychology.* 197F *13,* 552-564.

Cass, R., & Edney, J. J. The commons dilemma: A simulation testing the effects of resource visibility and territorial division. *Human Ecology,* 1978, 6, 371-386.

Edney, J. J. and Harper, C. S. The commons dilemma: A review of contributions from psychology. *Environmental Management,* 1978, *2,* 491-507.

Edney, J. J.. & Harper, C. S. The effects of information in a resource management problem: A social trap analog. *Human Ecology,* 1978, 6, 387-395(a).

Edney, J. J., & Harper, C. S. Heroism in a resource crisis: A simulation study. *Environmental Management,* 1978, *2.* 523-527(b).

Hardin, G. The tragedy of the commons. *Science,* 1968, *162,* 1243-1 248.

Watzke, C. E., Dana, I. M., Doktor, R. H., & Rubenstein, F. D. An experimental study of individual vs. group interest. *Acta Sociologica* 1972, *15*, 366-370.

978-0-595-36000-0
0-595-36000-9

Printed in the United States
44036LVS00005B